*F*OREVER FAITHFUL

A STUDY OF
FLORENCE BALLARD AND THE SUPREMES

by

Rand

Renaissance Sound and Publications   San Francisco, CA

1999 published by Renaissance Sound and Publications

ISBN: 0-943485-03-7
Library of Congress Catalog Card Number: 98-92257

Renaissance Sound and Publications
340 Hayes Street, Suite 607
San Francisco, CA 94102
(415) 621-0549
www.rnaisance.aol.com

Second Edition
Original cover design by Richard Zybert Graphics, San Francisco
back cover photo courtesy of Linda Champion
Typography by Printz, San Francisco
Special Thanks to Thomas Ingrassia for his contribution of the additional
photographs and essay.

Based on a thesis submitted to the Faculty of the Graduate School of the
University of Maryland in partial fulfillment of the requirements for the degree of
Master Arts, 1983.

Manufactured in the United States

Looking Back, 1998

Thirty years ago on a bright, cold December Saturday when the streets of Detroit still bustled with Christmas shoppers of every race and class, I made my usual trip downtown from the suburbs. The first stop was on Woodward Avenue at the huge newsstand in Kern's Square, to my right was the 25 story J.L. Hudson department store. The newstand was manned by three or four men hawking papers ranging from the Detroit Free Press to the Racing Forum and some mildly adult "girly" magazines. I always planned these trips to coincide with the biweekly release of Soul! Newspaper. I needed to find out what was up with all my favorite groups. Of course, I needed a Supremes news fix and hoped that there might be a glimmer of news on Florence. Just to sustain the jazzed excitement of being downtown, I would space out my activities on those sojourns, buy the paper and save reading it until lunch.

I loved going downtown in those years, to be a part of all the possibilities of life pulsing through the streets. Oh, there had been the riots the year before, but we were healing from those with insight and understanding, I felt. The changes would make us closer, it was Age of Aquarius.

Florence had signed with ABC Records the previous spring and already one single had been released. Aside from a small mention in the Detroit papers, that single was never heard from again. During the summer, Scott Regan, a local disc jockey from WKNR, ran a small mention in his teen beat column about

Florence having had an extensive recording session in New York. When Flo was the featured personality on the cover of "Detroit" in October of 1968, Barbara Holliday reviewed the second single "Love Ain't Love" as a good belting number. For weeks, I looked for the single without any luck. None of the stations played it and no stores carried it. Finally, on the cold December day, two months after it was released, I found the black label 45rpm in the record department of S.S. Kresge, the dime store, in downtown Detroit. I couldn't wait to get it home and hear it. It was a hit in my house, but that was it.

The record died and so did Flo's recording career. The following five or six years contained the elements of a Greek tragedy played out in the press, business offices, and court rooms. But on that day, standing in the middle of Kern's Square, I could look left on Woodward and see the Henry and Edsel Ford Auditorium, home of the Detroit Symphony, eight blocks away and turning right to look up Woodward the same distance was the Fox Theatre, which on that Saturday was home of the Motown Revue. The historic 16 blocks of Woodward that separated the two buildings, represented the entire career of Florence Ballard, and in many ways, The Supremes and Motown Records. Her first concert performances had been at the Fox and her last one was at Ford Auditorium.

Long years after her death, the pros and cons of Florence's life and career have filled chapters, been voiced on talk shows, posted on the websites, typed about in chat rooms and strained friendships. Unfortunately, many of the opinions were based on second-hand information, and the blessing of 20/20 hindsight. Several years ago, unauthorized tapes of Flo's "extensive" recording sessions began to surface. A letter writing campaign was directed to MCA Records[the current owners of the ABC library] encouraging the release of the songs, but nothing came of this. The comments on the quality of recordings varied from over enthusiastic to under whelmed. What was missing was perspective.

Florence was young when the sessions took place. The type of material she was singing ranged from a spirited Impossible Dream and Love Ain't Love and a passable Yesterday. These choices were made at the start of a career, and not intended to be the lasting legacy of a founding member of The Supremes. The better ending of the story would have Florence going on to record many albums with songs culled from the classics of popular music. Imagine Florence doing the Dinah Washington song book, or Gershwin's Summertime. We'd all be looking back on that first album with the same attitude we have toward the Meet the Supremes album knowing that the Rodgers and Hart album was yet to come or when we hear Meet the Beatles and marvel over the Sgt. Peppers album. Could she have done it? I think so.

Thirty years after buying Love Ain't Love (a song I still love), I was actually able to buy a Florence Ballard song on a cd in a Virgin Record store in San Francisco. MCA records had a change of heart. Remarkably, her first single, It Doesn't Matter How I Say It, was included in a collection of performances by other "soulful divas" including Dionne Warwick, Martha Reeves, Gladys Knight and Freda Payne. After all these years, in this small gesture, a mainstream record company finally recognized Florence's talent as equal to that of these other fine vocalists. This attention is something long denied by her home label, Motown, even now. This single release is, perhaps, the most any of us who are fans of Florence, Diana and Mary can hope for. Was it enough? I will never know. Sometimes I just wonder, what could have happened in that hopeful world of 1968?

The one thing I have realized in all these years is that whatever the critics and pundits have to say about Florence, she was and is a star. How else can you explain the continuing interest in the person and her story? This is something that probably would have surprised and pleased Florence. I can see her acknowledging it with a wink, a smile and a nod to all of us!

My own thanks are in order to all the readers of the first edition of this book and made this second edition possible. The first edition was presented at the first Florence Ballard Tribute in Los Angeles and it has been a remarkable eleven year journey since then. I again thank Tom Ingrassia for his friendship and contribution of documenting the history of The Supremes during the last 25 years. Carl Feurbacher for his dedication to Mary Wilson and all the fans. Through my interest in Florence, I have met and made wonderful friends: J. Randy Taraborrelli, David Ritz, Gil Lucero, Sharon Moore, Stephen White, Marty Robinson, Jon Chusid, Alice Manica, Nick Strange, Kevin Norwood, Dan Verona, Joe Chism, Paul and Diane Orleman. I want to acknowledge my Supreme friends who aren't here anymore: Alan Poe, Gary Oleszko (my pal from those Detroit days), John Culver, Bruce Robinson and Bob Berry. My special thanks also goes to Barbara Rose Brooker (my writing muse), my mom and my brother; each has been a constant source of encouragement. Lastly, my thanks go to Mary Wilson for her friendship and inspiration.
Randall Wilson
San Francisco, 1998

Foreword, 1998

Eleven years have passed since I wrote that forward for the first edition of <u>Forever Faithful!</u> Much has happened in those eleven years. Fortunately, we now have access to a wider range of Florence Ballard's recorded legacy. Recent releases by Motown have included some previously unreleased material with Flo singing lead. Bootleg copies of Flo's ill-fated ABC recording sessions have been circulating underground for several years. In January, 1988, Flo's daughter, Lisa, accepted her mother's lifetime achievement award from the Rock and Roll Hall of Fame. Along with Diana and Mary, Flo received a long-overdue star on the Hollywood Walk of Fame in 1994. And, just this month, it was announced that the original Supremes have been elected to the first class of inductees in the Vocal Group Hall of Fame. So, while the basic facts about Florence's life and death have not changed in the intervening years, hopefully our appreciation of her place not only in Motown's history, but also in pop music history, women's history and American history, has changed. And, while other books have been publish purporting to tell Florence Ballard's story, Randall Wilson is one of the few authors who has based his work on documented facts.

Despite these recent accolades, however, Florence Ballard has not received the same level of recognition from the media as have many of her fallen contemporaries. A recent **USA Today** article chronicled the continuing sales appeal of deceased artists including Mama Cass Elliot and Frankie Lymon. Florence Ballard was not included in this list of more than 15 deceased 1960s performers whose records continue to sell well after their deaths. It is unfortunate that Flo's contributions to pop music have been so completely overshadowed.

As a member of the most successful female group in music history, Florence Ballard deserves to be included in any list of pop music legends. In fact, having sung on 10 Number One records, she deserves a place at the top of the list--along side John Lennon and Elvis Presley. Let's face it--The Beatles and The Supremes were THE pop music icons of the 1960s.

The fairy tale (turned nightmare) story that Florence Ballard created with The Supremes is as powerful today as it was in 1959. With her big, Aretha Franklin-like, soulful, soprano voice, Florence Ballard--along with Mary Wilson--created the distinctive background vocals that made The Supremes so special and set them apart from all the other girl groups. The Supremes were not merely a lead singer with faceless, nameless backup singers. The Supremes were a cohesive unit, each member a star in her own right. The world fell in love with a TRIO of singers, and Florence Ballard shares in the rich musical legacy of The Supremes as much as Diana Ross and Mary Wilson.

The potency of Florence Ballard's legacy is evidenced by the continuing popularity of the Broadway musical, "Dreamgirls," whose central character, Effie, is patterned after Florence Ballard. And Motown obviously feels there is much life, vibrancy and power left in the original Supremes' catalog, as evidenced by its continuing reissues of greatest hits packages. Even today--40 years after the group's founding--all new female vocal groups are automatically compared with The Supremes. They set the bar high and together established a standard unparalleled in music history. The image that Florence Ballard created with The Supremes has become indelible. In the broader scope of history, however, Florence Ballard and The Supremes represent much more. The rise of The Supremes coincided with the civil rights movement in America. The Supremes' presence as highly visible, successful African-Americans made a considerable impact on the times. And, while not directly responsible for the civil rights movement, Florence Ballard, with The Supremes, did help to change Americans' attitudes about people of color.

With The Supremes, Florence Ballard was a trendsetter. She helped to break down the racial barriers and to open the doors for the African-American artists who would follow. The Supremes were the first African-American singing group to play Lincoln Center--while they were still living in the Projects! They were the first to play New York's Copacabana and Las Vegas. Long before it was in vogue for performers to do product endorsements, The Supremes endorsed Coca-Cola. They had their own brand of white bread on the market. Florence Ballard--all of Motown's female artists, for that matter-- represented a positive image of successful African-American women in society.

Their impact was as far reaching as was The Beatles'. As Mary Wilson has said many times, "Our success was not about the music. It was about what we represented. We were the American Dream come true, rags to riches. We changed the way the world saw black women. We were heroes to people. For black people especially, we became everyone's sister or daughter.

Blacks didn't have too many heroes in those days. But we gave people pride in themselves."

Florence Ballard truly is one of the greatest legends of music history and, as such, she deserves the recognition in death that was denied her during her life. At Flo's funeral in 1976, Mary Wilson's parting words to her friend and singing partner were, "Don't worry, Flo. I'll take care of it. We is terrific." Since the media and her record companies have all but forgotten Florence Ballard, it is up to her fans--and people like Mary Wilson and Randall Wilson--to keep her memory and her legacy alive.

And with this second edition of Florence's story, Randall Wilson goes a long way toward achieving that goal.

Thomas Ingrassia
Holden, Massachusetts
October 6, 1998

FOREWORD

Florence Ballard was a superstar at age twenty—the toast of two continents. By the time she was twenty-five, her career was over and she lived a forgotten life. At thirty, she was again a headline attraction, only this time because she was living on welfare. And she died at thirty-two. Florence Ballard was too young to die. Few performers have suffered so much, paid such a high price for a career, or had so few pleasant memories of fame as Florence Ballard.

Of course, Florence Ballard was the founding member of the most successful American singing group of all time. She was with The Supremes during their glory years — 1964 to 1967, when they were non-stop hit-makers and still sisters. Even though she was "star in the background" [to borrow a phrase from Mary Wilson], Flo's vocal prowess shone through like a beacon, overshadowing and perhaps intimidating the smaller, reedier sound of the more highly touted Supreme Diana Ross. Yet, despite her talent and her contributions to making Motown Records the top black-owned record company, Florence Ballard is perhaps best remembered by many as the tragic loser of The Supremes.

Certainly her life contained all the elements of a classic Greek tragedy. Hers was the ultimate rags-to-riches-to-rags story. But a loser? I think not. It would be easy to trace Florence's life through her music. Indeed, she did seem to live the lyrics of many of The Supremes' biggest hits. "I Hear a Symphony," she sang, but her life became "Nothing But Heartaches," and "Reflections." Such an assessment would be far too trite, however. As Randall Wilson proves in this, the first work to focus exclusively on her story, there was much more substance to Florence's short life. What Randall presents here is Flo's story of laughter, tears, and sorrow — facts gleaned from hours of exhaustive research and interviews.

Florence Ballard was indeed supreme. She was strong,

yet perhaps too vulnerable. During her life, she was wounded more than once. Although hurt, she always managed to pick herself up and move on. "To thine own self be true" was the key to the triumph and tragedy of Florence; it was the way she tried to live, no matter what others thought, for better or worse. Was it fate that transformed Florence from one of three Black American Princesses, as Mary Wilson dubbed The Supremes, to a welfare mother? Or was it, as she charged in her lawsuit a "malicious conspiracy" — against which she could never prevail, no matter how brave or righteous her struggle — that led to her downfall and death?

Mary Wilson has said that "dreams don't die, people just stop dreaming." Certainly The Supremes were the ultimate embodiment of Florence's dream. Perhaps Flo did let her dream die when she left The Supremes, but her dream continues to live in the heart and soul of every Supremes' fan around the world. It binds us all together, it is now our dream. Florence can be proud of that accomplishment.

Florence Ballard and life waged a bittersweet contest for supremacy and ultimately they destroyed each other. Yet, during her struggle, Florence made some very beautiful music. This is Flo's true legacy, and it can never be taken from her.

Tom Ingrassia
Worcester, Massachusetts

DEDICATION

This thesis is dedicated to my mother, Jerry Wilson
and my father, Norman R. Wilson, M.D.

ACKNOWLEDGEMENTS

Diana Ross, Mary Wilson, and Florence Ballard sang with a spirit of youth and hope that captured the heart of America. The Supremes arrived at a time when the country was looking for some bright faces. The Supremes bridged the gap between parents and their children; everyone could enjoy listening to them or seeing them in performance. Although their songs were not outstanding musically, the aura of The Supremes themselves rose above the compositions. The trio was also the pride of my hometown. This was the dream of Berry Gordy, Jr. who, with his family and associates, worked toward creating the Motown Sound of Detroit.

This case study examines the events which lead to The Supremes' stardom and the failure of Florence Ballard to achieve that same stardom for herself. The business side of the recording industry is not as glamorous as the public side. It is not my intention to remove the glamour but to reveal how it is created and destroyed. This study evolved out of respect for Berry Gordy, the Motown Record Corporation, and The Supremes.

Personal thanks are extended to several people for helping to make this study possible: the late Florence Ballard for letting me know it was possible; Mary Wilson, Robert Bateman, Rosilee Trombley, John Young, and Arnold Stone for taking the time to be interviewed; Max Wilson and Al Abrams for their encouragement; and Mollie Wilson, Linda Champion, and Steven Ramey for their technical assistance. Special thanks go to Dr. Michael DuMonceau and the faculty of the University of Maryland division of Radio, Television and Film for their academic guidance.

Randall Wilson
Detroit, Michigan

AUTHOR'S NOTES

In June, 1963, my sister Mollie won a package of records in a radio station contest. We waited for the package to arrive hoping that Sam Cooke's hit "It's Another Saturday Night" would be in it. It wasn't. There were nine flops and one hit. Now I can't remember the hit, but the record that became a hit for us was a white label audition copy of "You Bring Back Memories" by a group called The Supremes. The label with the map was all too familiar for this family of four misplaced Detroit kids in Chattanooga, Tennessee. We could almost pick out our neighborhood on the label. "You bring back memories of all those days gone by." Oh, we loved that song.

During the next several years, Detroit was becoming famous, not for cars, but for music. It made me proud to be from the Motor City. When we moved back to Detroit, Motown in Motown was a personal thing. The chance of seeing Michigan's most exportable singers, as the governor called The Supremes, was as close as going to Hudson's downtown, maybe. But The Supremes and the other famous Motowners were accessible. They sang on the local television shows, at the State Fair, and still shopped at Hudson's. In school the conversations ran from "Who is your favorite Beatle?" to "Who is your favorite Supreme?" My favorite was Florence. I remember when they were in the news promoting white bread and Coke. In Detroit, we knew when The Supremes were on tour, or in town. The disk jockeys knew them. Scotty Regan of WKNR wrote the album notes to *The Supremes Sing Holland Dozier Holland.*

I remember the day I came home from Bob-Lo Amusement Park, which sometimes had a Motown group performing on the boat that sailed down the Detroit River to the park, when my dad showed me a small article which said that

Florence was leaving The Supremes. At the time I thought it was crazy. How could The Supremes be Supremes if one is replaced? They were sisters and Detroiters. Three weeks later, at the Michigan State Fair, a group called "Diana Ross and the Supremes" performed with Cindy Birdsong, who seemed nice, instead of Florence Ballard. But it was now "Diana Ross and the Supremes" and it was all changed.

After August 1967 The Supremes were gone. The three singers from the Motor City who became sisters were beyond the Motown family we all adopted and beyond Detroit, which meant business in the record world. That Florence was not there was not important as long as the Supreme image was maintained. But for this Supremes' fan, it was the individuals which made the image. In 1975, when Flo's story again hit the papers, I contacted her about a radio program on The Supremes. My dream was of being Flo's producer . I hoped she would be interested in the radio show. She wrote back and said "yes." I was thrilled. She also requested borrowing my copy of "Love Ain't Love." Before the show was completed, however, my father called to say Flo had died. The radio project never happened, but the dream did not die.

In 1982, I proposed developing Florence Ballard's career situation into a case study for my Master's thesis in the Department of Communication Arts at the University of Maryland. It was my good fortune to have an understanding advisor who took on my project. I returned to the Motor City and relearned what it meant to be a Detroiter. The spirit of the people there helped me to write this story about someone who is still very special in their hearts. A lady at the Detroit Public Library saw an article on a microfilm reader and said, "Oh, that's when Florence died," as though to say she lost a friend. And in a way she did. Detroit is a city that has had its share of problems, but it has always pulled together. Everyone there loved The Supremes. The Motown 25th Anniversary was not in Detroit; when Diana said that everyone came back, she was wrong. Not everyone could come back; Motown did not comeback, but everyone can be remembered.

So, this book is a tribute to those artists and the hometown fans who haven't always been remembered when the lights got too bright, when the press releases got too lofty, and when that elusive star of fame faded to black. Just remember that there were three girls who shared a dream, made it happen and it was their star together which shined. Florence Ballard, Mary Wilson, and Diana Ross were The Supremes.

Randall Wilson

Special thanks to Tom and Barbara Ingrassia, Linda Champion, Alan White, Richard Sotelo, Steve Ramey, Clark Coffee of H. S. Dakin, and everyone at Printz for their assistance in the publication of Forever Faithful.

The Supremes with the Jimmy Wilkins Band
at the Michigan State Fair, 1965. (l-r) Florence Ballard,
Mary Wilson, Diana Ross

Florence Ballard, 1968

Chapter I

Five thousand people crowded in and near New Bethel Baptist Church in Detroit, Michigan on Friday, February 27, 1976. The Reverend C. L. Franklin, father of singer Aretha Franklin, conducted a funeral service inside, while the Detroit Police maintained the crowd outside. This was the funeral service for Florence Ballard. The news of Florence's death was carried nationally by the wire services; one year earlier she was living on a limited income in obscurity. The week before her funeral, however, thousands of Detroiters paid their respects to this woman who had died of cardiac arrest at the age of thirty-two. What was all this outpouring of attention about? Florence Ballard was a Supreme!

Florence Ballard, Mary Wilson, and Diana Ross were The Supremes. They were high school friends who sang at record hops and parties in the late 1950s; they lived in public housing then. By 1966, The Supremes owned their own homes and gave sequin-studded performances from Tokyo to London, New York to Los Angeles. They were nick-named The Sweethearts of America when the Beatles were known as the Lads from Liverpool. Between 1964 and 1967, The Supremes recorded seven consecutive Number-one million selling records. This had never been accomplished by any recording artists, not even the Beatles.

The Supremes were the top rated act for a newly formed black-owned recording company in Detroit. Motown Records, short for motor town, was a total production facility which recorded and directed the promotion and management of rhythm and blues musicians like a musical General Motors. The owner of this company, Berry Gordy, Jr., brought the artists, writers and producers together in the most successful black recording company in the country. The Supremes were the stars of Motown in 1966.

In August 1967, the *Detroit Free Press* announced that Supreme Florence Ballard was temporarily leaving the trio for a month of rest due to exhaustion. Flo Ballard, known as the quiet member of the group, sang background vocals

1

along with Mary Wilson. Motown publicity agents would not discuss the personnel change three weeks later when the group appeared at the Michigan State Fair in Detroit. Cindy Birdsong, who bore a striking physical resemblance to Flo, became the newest member of the trio. The name of the trio was changed to "Diana Ross and the Supremes" in August 1967. During the next two years, The Supremes' act became a showcase for Diana Ross. The recordings made by the group emphasized Ross as a soloist rather than a group lead singer.

Flo Ballard never returned to The Supremes. She signed a contract with ABC Records in 1968, but this attempt to become a soloist failed. In November 1969, when Motown publicity announced that Diana Ross was leaving The Supremes for a solo career, Flo Ballard's career was an artistic and commercial failure.

This study of The Supremes and Florence Ballard answers questions regarding Flo's recording career with The Supremes and as a soloist. The Supremes were an outstanding musical phenomenon in popular music from 1964 until 1969. Both Diana Ross and Florence Ballard left the group to pursue solo careers, but only Ross achieved national recognition. This study examines the related areas of talent development, artist management, artist promotion, and contractual considerations of the recording industry to understand why Flo's solo career failed. This will be brought out by answering questions which surrounded the failure of Flo's career.

In answering these questions, it is necessary to study the history of Flo Ballard's involvement with Motown Records prior to signing with ABC Records. A historical structure was chosen to provide a body of research in this case. The subjects of artist development, management and promotion are discussed in relation to the chronology of events in Florence Ballard's professional career. Newspaper articles, reviews, press interviews, and court records are sources of information utilized to document this case study.

At this time [1982] there is only one analytical study of Motown Records, Benjaminson's *Story of Motown*. This book discusses Flo Ballard with regard to her position as a Supreme, but does not touch upon her career after leaving the trio. Alan Betrock's *Girl Groups: The Story of a Sound* has a summary of The Supremes with one sentence devoted to Ballard's solo career. James Haskin's biography of Diana Ross, *I'm Gonna Make You Love Me*, treatment of Flo Ballard tends to be limited without insight to the difficulties she experienced after leaving The Supremes. Because there is limited literature available which focuses on Florence Ballard, this study may be of value to biographers of Supremes Mary Wilson and Diana Ross.

The history of Florence Ballard's rise and fall from stardom in music is but one incident in the recording industry. Although her solo career was a failure, an awareness of the decisions which guided her may be expanded for artists, producers, and agents for recreating success and preventing failure in their own careers.

"Honey, we is Terrific!"
(l-r) Florence Ballard, Mary Wilson, Diana Ross

3

The Supremes
(above) an early publicity still of
the "no hit" Supremes, 1963.

(left) The Supremes in a famous
glamour shot, 1965.

[photos courtesy of

Thomas Ingrassia]

4

Chapter II

Detroit was settled by French explorers as a Great Lakes region trading post. Antoine Cadillac established the Detroit River fur trading settlement in 1701. Detroit evolved into a larger community which traded not only fur, but iron ore and limestone from the northern reaches of Michigan. The French influence was felt in Detroit well after the American Revolution. *Detroit News* writer Malcolm Bingay attributed the city's lasting cultural heritage to three men: Father Gabriel Richard, a French priest and scholar; the Reverend John Montieth; and Judge Augustus Woodward. These three men established debate societies, schools, and libraries. In 1801, they founded the University of Michigan.

The Detroit River, which played an important role in the economic development of the city, became politically significant in the first half of the 19th century. The international border between Canada and the United States is this river. Detroit was the last United States city on the underground railway in the abolitionist movement before the Civil War. Between 1829 and 1862, approximately forty thousand slaves passed through Detroit to seek freedom in Canada. While the number of permanent black residents remained small, the progression of blacks through Detroit added to its cultural and social variation. By the turn of the century, Detroit had a black population of four thousand.

The modern era of Detroit began in the 1900s with the expansion of the steel and automobile industries. Waves of immigrants came to the city in search of employment added diversity and strength to Detroit. The European immigration of Polish, German, and Italian workers declined after World War I; black workers from the south responded to the need for industrial laborers. The rapid growth and prosperity of the automobile industry made Detroit a city of hope, a leader in higher wages for industrial workers based on a philosophy of practicality with an ability to get a job done. Union strength tied the workers together within this common goal. The Automotive Council demonstrated this ability most dramatically during World War II; Detroit ceased car production and built war munitions ranging from jeeps and tanks to bombers.

The post World War II automotive industry boom caused metro-Detroit to grow beyond its own boundaries into three suburban counties. Detroit is the only major U.S. metropolis to have a single, dominating industry. Twenty-eight percent of the metropolitan area work force was involved with automobile production in 1950; this figure does not include those working the automobile feeder industries. While the automobile industry affects every aspect of the metropolitan economy and lends a similitude throughout these communities, there is an underlying cultural contrast among the populous. The influx of ethnic groups has created a cultural quilt of entertainment tastes.

Detroit's reputation as a national music center began in 1905 when Jerome H. Remick formed the Remick Music Publishing Company. His company published over fifty thousand songs in its twenty-three year history. Remick was responsible for publishing songs still popular today: "By The Light of The Silvery Moon;" "On Moonlight Bay;" and "I'm Forever Blowing Bubbles." In 1918, Remick assisted in the organization of the Detroit Symphony Orchestra under the baton of Ossip Gabrilowitsch, a famous Russian pianist. The influence of this decision played a part in the production of Motown Records. Gabrilowitsch furthered Detroit's musical reputation nationally with the creation of the Interlochen Music Academy, the building of Orchestra Hall, and the national radio broadcast of live symphonic music in 1931.

As the white population moved from the city to the suburbs, Detroit became a leading black city. Black oriented entertainment and recreational and commercial facilities were established during the post-war years to serve this growing community. After the Detroit Symphony moved from Orchestra Hall, the hall became the Paradise Theatre from 1941 until 1951. As the Paradise, it was a national showplace for leading black musicians including Billie Holiday, Earl Hines, Count Basie, Lionel Hampton, Sammy Davis, Jr., and Pearl Bailey.

6

Local black talent emerged during this time of growth as well. Jazz singer Della Reese and harpist Dorothy Ashby came to prominence in Detroit in the 1950s. A major radio outlet for Detroit's black community was WCHB-AM. This station went on air in 1955. This station and WJLB, another black station, consistently played releases from Motown Records and other black record labels. The top-forty radio stations in the city, CKLW, WKNR, and WXYZ, followed the black stations' lead in programming Motown songs.

The influence of Detroit's automotive production, coupled with the rise of the city's black community, gave way to the development of low-income housing projects. The Brewster Douglass Projects was one such development on the near east side of Detroit. It was from this particular project that Florence Ballard, Mary Wilson, and Diane Ross rose to international stardom.

The Ballards came to Detroit from Mississippi in 1929 when the automobile plants were expanding. Jessie Ballard was a guitarist but found work at Chevrolet. Florence Ballard was born in 1943, one of twelve children. She learned to sing from her father. When Jessie Ballard died, the family encouraged her to continue her musical education in school.

Florence talked about her life for *Look* in 1966. "When I was small, I remember walking to school with holes in my shoes. I hid them from my mother. I walked real flat so nobody could see the holes. The funny thing was that everybody thought I was stuck-up because I walked with my head up. I still have a great, proud walk, and people still think I'm stuck-up. At school, I was never tardy because I loved it so. I had blonde hair from the age of three. Everybody called me Blondie. I was a good student, always interested in music, even then. My teacher would say, 'Blondie, drop your jaw, breathe from the stomach,' and my jaws felt paralyzed, but all this work paid off." One of her friends in elementary school was Mary Wilson, who lived in the projects.

Mary Wilson moved into the projects at the age of eleven after being reared as the adopted daughter of her aunt and uncle in a southwest Detroit middle-class black neighborhood. When Mary Wilson's natural father died, her mother moved to Detroit from Greenville, Mississippi, bringing two younger children with her. Although Mary found this move confusing, the new experience of living with her family taught Wilson how to be with people, yet guard her privacy.

Flo Ballard and Mary sang in a church choir together and also performed in a talent show at school. Their friends included Betty Travis and Barbara Martin. Because all four young girls lived in the same neighborhood and shared an interest in music, they remained friends even though each went to a different high school.

In 1959, Motown Records evolved out of Detroit's musical milieu. Berry Gordy, Jr., the company's founder, guided it from a small independent local label to an internationally important force in popular music. Germane to the company history and its artists is the history of Gordy. Detroit's "3-D Record Mart," owned by Gordy, his first venture in the music business, failed. Through this initial endeavor, however, Gordy met record distributors who later assisted him in starting his record company. Detroit was a musically active city with small record companies that served the local musicians. Through the record store enterprise, night club contacts, and talent competition observation, Gordy was in touch with key people in the popular black music field in Detroit. After the failure of the "3-D Record Mart," Gordy became an assembler with an automobile manufacturer, learning mass production in the process.

The collapse of the record store did not end Gordy's involvement with the music business. He spent his after-hours song writing. The songs were eventually recorded by Detroit singers Barrett Strong, Marv Johnson, and Jackie Wilson. Wilson's 1958 recording of Gordy's "Lonely Tear-drops" was among Wilson's most popular. These recordings by Barrett Strong and Jackie Wilson were licensed to larger record labels for national distribution from which Gordy received a small royalty. As an independent songwriter, Gordy was encouraged to write and produce for other musicians.

Gordy met a young writer/singer, William "Smokey" Robinson, in 1959. Robinson's singing group, The Miracles, auditioned with the hope of being produced by Gordy. Robinson had a notebook of songs, all rejected by Gordy. The songs did not have the structure or strong story line that Gordy wanted; however, he and Robinson began working together. The Miracles' first release, a Gordy-Robinson song entitled "Gotta Job," was distributed on the New York END label. The second release, "Bad Girl," was on the Chicago CHESS label. Prompted by Robinson, Gordy began his own label after these two releases. The first MOTOWN label record was Marv Johnson's "Come to Me" in 1959. Motown distributed the record locally; United Artists distributed it nationally. Thus, the Motown Record Corporation was launched in 1959.

Motown's early achievements were marked by their first million record selling single of "Shop Around" by The Miracles. The company was a small operation, however, and the problems of distribution had to be overcome. Local distribution in Southeast Michigan was handled by the company; regional and national distribution was managed by independent companies. These independent distributors would overextend themselves, leaving Motown with outstanding accounts receivable. Gordy's sister, Loucye Wakefield, was made vice president of management to oversee this area. Motown established four labels, MOTOWN, GORDY, TAMLA, and SOUL, to increase the potential of concurrent radio promotion. Barney Ales was hired to manage Motown distribution.

Gordy and Ales met in 1958 when Gordy was producing for Marv Johnson. Ales had opened the Detroit Warner Brothers distributorship before Motown went national. Ales knew national distributors when he became head of Motown distribution. The entire company and studios were located in two houses on West Grand Boulevard, a formerly fashionable residential area ten blocks from General Motor's corporate headquarters. Ales described the organization as a family during the early years. The Motown "family" employed ten members of Gordy's family. One Motown musician, Junior Walker, said of Motown, "Berry was the head of the family. He was like the father and everybody takes their bow to the father and listens to him."

Detroit's musical community became aware of Motown in 1960 and 1961 as The Miracles gained popularity. Motown representatives visited talent shows to hear groups before inviting them to audition for possible recording contracts. Three female groups performing regularly in Detroit were the Andantes, Del-Phis, and the Primettes. Occasionally, these groups would record background vocals at Motown's Hitsville studios.

Gordy's new organization was both successful and efficient. *New York Times'* Richard Lingeman described Gordy as a napoleonic perfectionist who expected nothing less from his employees. Under his supervision, a song might be recorded twenty or more times before meeting with his approval. Pressure was placed upon writers, producers, and musicians to create only the best possible records. All recordings had to be approved by Gordy, making competition strong among producers and musicians for a polished product. A greater challenge for producers was winning Gordy's favor for a record release. He encouraged competition by tying salaries to the numbers of hits a producer had. Once a record was released, it had a one-in-three chance of being a hit.

The Gordy formula of a perfect record was characterized by producer Norman Whitfield as being unique. "Every producer is free to produce for any artist under contract. No one has the exclusive right to lock-up one artist because he had the previous hit record. In other words, his best record goes out." Whitfield came to Motown after working for several smaller companies; within four months at Motown, he had a hit record with his production of Marvin Gaye's "Pride and Joy' in 1963. Producers recorded the music tracks for a song and tried several groups before a final decision was made on the production. If the song did not suit one group, singers were interchanged while the music tracks remained the same. This freedom to work with all the Motown artists increased the producers' chances of having a hit. According to Gordy, the company would have failed financially without a hit record each year; profits went back into the business. Retrospectively, Gordy called it 'foolish' but worth the risk.

Independent record companies, such as Motown, depended on selling hit records to cover the expense of production. An independent label had to sell approximately twenty-thousand units to cover these costs; only thirty percent of the records released in the 1960s achieved this. Large companies could absorb the losses through sales of sound track albums and recordings of well established artists. By concentrating on potential hit single records, Motown was able to survive during its first four years. The limited releases of songs by The Miracles, Marvelettes, Marvin Gaye, and Mary Wells from 1959 through 1963 boosted Motown's 1963 earnings to $4.5 million.

During Motown's formative years, 1960 through 1964, some producers came to the company as writers or singers. Besides Smokey Robinson and Berry Gordy, other producers included Brian Holland, Eddie Holland, and Robert Bateman. Bateman described how he came to Motown: "First I was an artist, I was with the SatinTones. I didn't come as a SatinTone, I came as an artist in another group. I forgot what we called ourselves. I think the "El Capitanos" and we auditioned for Berry and he didn't like the group. But I think he was looking for a bass voice to do background and we were the Raeber voices. Anyway, it was Rae and Berry and they had the Raeber writing service and did writing for Jackie Wilson and Marv Johnson, I know you are familiar with them. We were the background voices on all those— Mary Wells, Barrett Strong. You know all the old stuff. We had the background on it.... And from there I started to write and then we formed the group the SatinTones." Neither group lasted, but Bateman stayed to became a background singer, producer-writer, and recording engineer. Eddie Holland recorded a solo album and a few singles before writing and producing.

Bateman and Brian Holland collaborated as producers for Motown's first girl-group, the Marvelettes. Together they wrote under the pen name of "Brianbert." The teams would write the songs which were recorded in Motown's own studios. The rhythm, string, and brass instrumental tracks, provided by Detroit Symphony Orchestra musicians [some-

11

times known as The San Remo Strings had a hit single "Hungry for Love" in 1965], would be recorded before the singers were brought into the studios. The producers knew in advance the type of sound they wanted from the singers. Because Motown owned its recording facilities, producers could record a bulk of instrumental tracks for all the groups. This enabled the company to have consistent public exposure and maintain sales momentum.

Recording acts were molded to the standards of excellence set by the corporation. Production policy and creative rivalry among producers meant that singers were given little freedom to decide what was recorded. Singers who did not fit into this structure were not promoted. Because of Gordy's emphasis of releasing only potential hit material, once a group or singer had a hit, other producers would submit production requests for that group. Bateman continued, "Basically, we'd [the producers] come up with something of a hit. The artists had little say in the choice of material at that time. It was strictly from the producers. We'd lay the tracks and the artists had to sing what we had for them. And they had to sing it the way we wanted it sung. I am just being frank and honest with you. Later on, once I did get into the art, I did see that the artist was given a little consideration as far as the choice of materials. But I guess it was a successful way of doing it because the proof is in the pudding."

The young singers at Motown were untrained for professional stage appearances. Their musical experiences had been limited to high school and talent shows. The Marvelettes, for example, were in school in 1960 when Bateman brought them into the studios to record "Please, Mr. Postman" which, incidentally, was one of the Beatles' first records a few years later. The Marvelettes went on tour taking a tutor with them. Motown employed this young talent in the studios, but had to develop them into a publicly acceptable "product."

International Talent Management, Incorporated [I.T.M.I.] a subsidiary of the Motown Corporation, established a training program for their artists. Under the guidance of veteran band leader Maurice King, who had a long established reputation for his Flame Bar in Detroit, each group was groomed and polished for public appearances. One of the houses on the Boulevard became the training school in which classes were held on a regular schedule. Students were taught personal grooming, etiquette, and diction which was followed by a program of stage development: if a number required a performer to be seated at a piano; instruction was given to do so properly. Every movement and line said in the act was planned and rehearsed to perfection. What was the Artist Development Program like? Supreme Mary Wilson: "What was like? It consisted of a lot of very talented people: they had choreographers; finishing school teachers for etiquette and things of that nature; also they had a music department where a lot of arrangers would teach harmony and songs and classic songs— whatever they (or he) thought was needed they would send to a particular person and that person would work with the artist. They worked with all of us and we learned a lot about choreography. Basically it was a finishing school at Motown. The program itself went on for quite a few years, in its heyday, lasted only about three years."

The Motown recording organization and the I.T.M.I. training were rigid and rigorous. The Artist Development Department would schedule each act, devise the artistic concept, and rehearse the performers. Each student was expected to perform to the same level of perfection that Gordy demanded of those making the recordings. King, like Gordy, was a tough disciplinarian who drilled the students until they were exhausted. There was little resistance to this training which made some of the students top-rated performers.

Martha Reeves came to Motown as a secretary in the Artist and Repertoire Department after being turned down for an audition. She had studied voice in a special high school program and had been in several singing groups before substituting for Mary Wells in a recording session. Martha Reeves was then signed to Motown as lead singer of "Martha and the Vandellas". She felt the demand of the training provided by the company was needed, "There was at one time a need for a modeling instructor who taught us how to walk properly and eat properly in case we were in the presence of someone we wanted to impress—just to know what was right. It was not forced on us, but being a young company they were very wise in doing that."

Artist Development was worth the effort for the artists and the company alike. The groups were able to perform in sophisticated nightclubs where only polished entertainment was expected. Glittering costumes and stylistic choreography became Motown artists' trademarks. Gordy worked toward making his acts appealing to a diversified audience. Without the training classes, these performers would have appeared as the high school amateurs they had been. Less organized recording companies did not make this investment on their artists and ultimately these singers did not enjoy long careers.

Gordy created his own touring musical showcase, "MotorTown Revues," once the acts were perfected. Sometimes the revues included non-Motown groups. These reviews gave the Motown artists an opportunity to know their competitors. The rivalry with other popular singers was further encouraged within Motown. Otis Williams, a member of the Motown quintet The Temptations, recalls the group's first out-of-town engagements: "The first place we performed out of Detroit was Cleveland and Gladys [Knight] and the Pips were on there. We felt we could hold our own until we saw Gladys and them come out on stage. They were dancing, doing this and that. We said, 'Fellows, we've got to go back to Detroit and do some more rehearsing.' So, we went and rehearsed and rehearsed. Then we went to Philadelphia; The Flamingoes were on the show. We watched them and the way they were moving. We packed up and came back to Detroit and rehearsed. Then we went back to Baltimore and Gladys and them were on the show that time; we pretty much held our own."

Weekly meetings began with a pep rally song about the Motown "family"; everyone in attendance was expected to sing. Gordy challenged the *family* with a question of "would you rather buy this record under review or a sandwich?" Awards were given to the best songwriter, producer, and singer. If the groups were on tour, they would strive to outshine one another on a shared bill. The "MotorTown Revues" would open with the newest or less popular act and close with the headlining act such as The Miracles. Tensions erupted from the demands of performance on these long tours. Marv Johnson remembers the girl-groups squabbling on tour. A chaperon, generally a parent, accompanied the girls.

In the 1960s, black entertainers did not have the same acceptance among white audiences as white entertainers. Gordy was aware of this situation and made his drive for perfection greater. Phil Spector, a white producer for other black singers including The Ronettes in the mid-1960s, commented that Motown gave their singers direction and material they needed to reach a wide audience. Singers without that support were not achieving the success found at Motown. Gordy's struggling company became the country's most prosperous producer of single records by 1964.

The elegant Supremes on one of many television appearances (l-r) Diana Ross, Mary Wilson, Florence Ballard.

The Supremes!
(l-r) Diana Ross, Mary Wilson, Florence Ballard

16

Chapter III

The year Smokey Robinson and The Miracles met Gordy, promoter Milton Jenkins began managing Florence Ballard as a soloist in addition to a male group, The Primes. Members in that group, Eddie Kendricks and Paul Williams who knew Florence Ballard, brought her to Jenkins' attention. She appeared as a soloist with the group, but Jenkins [who became Flo's brother-in-law] wanted a girl-group to complete the stage act. He asked Flo if she had any friends who might be interested in singing with her in a group. Flo asked Mary Wilson to join her. Even during their elementary school days they had talked of singing together. Two other friends, Barbara Martin and Betty Travis joined Flo and Mary to become The Primettes in 1959.

The group appeared in Detroit at dances and popular record-hops. Age, school, and family responsibilities prevented The Primettes from pursuing full time singing careers. Betty Travis left the group shortly after it was formed. On the advice of one of the Primes, Wilson asked Diane Ross to replace Betty as the fourth member. Diane Ross also lived in the Brewster Douglass Projects and attended yet another high school. Unlike Flo and Mary, both of whom studied voice in school, Diane had no formal training in music; she studied fashion design at Cass Technical High School. The lead vocals were shared among the four Primettes. Flo recalled for *Look*, "I was the one who got the whole thing started with our careers. I rounded up Mary, who rounded up Diana, and later on, I even picked the name, The Supremes. We used to hitchhike to record hops all around Detroit, not making a dime, and we used to call the fellows to pick us up if we couldn't get home."

Mary discussed those early years in Detroit: "We used to sing at The Twenty Grand, we did a lot of record hops at The Twenty Grand, and we used to work at 14th and Marquette. It was like a record hop building, like a disco today— and where else? We did The Roostertail night club and lots of unknown dances. We also did a lot of the state fairs in the

17

early days and we were in Canada." Did The Primettes get to know other pre-Motown groups? "Not really. The Temptations used to be The Distants, Otis Williams and The Distants, we knew them and worked with them quite a bit." Who else? "Martha and the Vandellas, they were singing—I would imagine they were singing around the same time we were in 1959—around Detroit. And were all in school then," she laughed.

The accomplishments of the Motown Record Corporation were well known among Detroiters when The Primettes were "conquering" Detroit, Mary recalled. "Well, Diana lived on the same street as Smokey and his family lived on...so when the group got together and decided we wanted to go to Motown. We tried to reach Smokey to see if he would listen to us...which he did and that was how we got to Motown." But the group was turned down by Motown producer Richard Morris. Diane's lead vocal at this audition was unimpressive. The Marvelettes, another Motown girl-group, had been signed and the company did not need a second group at this time. A smaller label, LuPine Records, did sign The Primettes to a limited contract, however. They worked as background singers for rhythm and blues singers Wilson Pickett and Eddie Floyd. LuPine recorded two singles for The Primettes featuring Mary Wilson's lead vocal. In spite of their failed bid with these records, the group stayed together.

The Primettes were ready to come back to Motown by late 1960. At that time, The Marvelettes had found success with Eddie Holland and Bateman's production of "Please, Mr. Postman." The next three Marvelettes songs on the TAMLA label were on the *Billboard* charts for a total of thirty-five weeks. Girl-groups on other labels were also having chart hits. Writer-producers such as Don Kirshner, Carole King, and Phil Spector were producing for The Crystals, The Ronettes, and The Cookies. This girl-group sound was gaining popularity in top-forty radio markets. This sound refers to a particular production technique and was not limited to just girl-groups.

Typically, a lead vocal was recorded over a background group vocal harmony of that lyric or a counterpoint lyric. The melody would be underscored with a constant four-beat rhythm section. While Bateman and Holland realized that girl-groups were beginning to compete on the radio chart and in record sales, Motown's share of this market was limited to The Marvelettes and soloist Mary Wells.

Mary Wells came to Motown as an aspiring songwriter through an audition arranged by Bateman. Her song "Bye, Bye Baby" written with Jackie Wilson in mind, was instead produced by Gordy as Wells' first release on the MOTOWN label. The Gordy style of a "perfect record" went into "Bye, Bye Baby" which he recorded more than twenty times before it was considered acceptable. Wells' early tough vocal on this song was later softened with producer Smokey Robinson's guidance. Wells recorded for Motown from 1960 until 1964, usually backed by the Andantes.

Gordy ordered more songs to be written for Wells who was becoming Motown's top soloist. Robinson became her producer; the Wells-Robinson partnership put Mary Wells on the charts four times in two years. She teamed with Marvin Gaye, toured with the Beatles, and achieved the Number-one record position in 1964 with "My Guy". Mary Wells, Motown's first female artist, was also their first recording artist to have a Number-one record.

Bateman recalled, "Actually, I am the one — it is hard for me because no one likes to ring his own bell— but I am the one who brought The Supremes in. Actually, they were brought in by another fellow, Richard Morris. And they were passed over. And actually I think it was because the girl sang through her nose. So Brian and I started to watch the charts and we started to see that— it was our opinion that girls' groups were starting to happen or started to happen. I remembered this girl-group which came through and were turned down and approached Berry with it. At the time they were minors and we were careful about getting involved with minors, especially girls. But I guess I had gained Berry's respect to the extent that if it was something I wanted to do, hey, it's my baby. And I went out and— they were Primettes and they were actually signed to another label at that time, but nothing was happening to them. I went out and got the girls and brought them in. Mrs. Edwards did the basic legal research and everything and got them out of their contracts and signed them to Motown." Although they were still minors under contract to LuPine, Esther Gordy Edwards arranged to end this contract.

Mary Wilson remembers, "Well, we went to audition for Motown in 1961— I think, I am not good with dates— anyway, we started recording there but did not have any hit records and we were in high school at that time. So we just decided to go out and get jobs— we weren't making any money— to supplement what we were doing. So Diana got a job at Hudson's Department Store and I also got a job at a record shop all around the same time." The girls took part time jobs after school to help pay for transportation costs to the studios and personal appearances. While Diane worked as a cafeteria bus girl at the downtown J. L. Hudson department store and Mary worked in the record store, Florence baby sat. Mary and Flo's mothers were supportive of their daughters' efforts to the point that their education did not suffer. Diane Ross's family was a little "touchy," according to Mary, when The Primettes became serious about singing. The advice given the group at the first Motown audition was for each member to finish high school and get more singing experience. The Primettes gained more experience, but only three finished high school. Florence dropped out of Northeastern High School in her senior year.

Believing the group's name was out of style, Gordy gave The Primettes one day to decide a new name. This was a common activity at Motown. According to Martha Reeves, Gordy would choose a name if a group could not decide: "When you have a record and it's supposed to be a hit, someone comes up and says, 'Ok, if you don't find a name in fifteen minutes,' someone like Berry Gordy, 'We are going to call you The Tillies.' So, we sat down and came up with 'Vandellas' as fast as we could."

The Primettes were treated no differently than Martha and the Vandellas. The girls went to company friends asking for suggestions. A secretary typed a list of potential names for the group from which Flo chose 'Supremes.' "At least I get credit for something," she remarked in a 1966 interview. Thus on January 15, 1961, Florence, Mary, Barbara and Diane began their Motown careers as The Supremes.

The Supremes' first single on the TAMLA label, "I Want A Guy," released late in 1961, was an uninspiring song featuring Diane; the song was a flop. After this first release, The Supremes became a trio when Barbara Martin left to get married. Motown did not replace Barbara and The Supremes continued to record as a trio and background singers.

Following in the Vandellas' footsteps, The Supremes sang background on Marvin Gaye's "Can I Get a Witness?" A series of writers produced material for The Supremes, but had no sales. The Supremes' second release, "Who's Lovin' You," written and produced by Smokey Robinson, did not fare any better than the first; however, the flip-side gained the attention of radio programmers in Detroit. Again Robert Bateman: "We tried to make Florence Ballard the original lead singer. I don't know if you know their first record, 'Buttered Popcorn', well that was Florence." "Buttered Popcorn," written by Gordy and Ales, featured Florence Ballard. Ales felt that this song's potential could put the Supremes on the national record charts, but Gordy did not let Ales promote the record. Mary Wilson: "There was some talk about it, but I am not really sure about it. But I do think that there was some talk that it was decided that was not the record to go with." It did, however, remain on regional playlists. In 1970, Ales told a Detroit radio interviewer, "A lot of people may not be familiar that originally The Supremes were four girls [until] after the first two records, one of which Berry and I wrote called 'Buttered Popcorn' and I keep trying to get released. So, let's play it tonight!"

If "Buttered Popcorn" had been promoted, the public would have identified Florence Ballard as the group's lead singer. Flo sang the unreleased "Save Me A Star", an up-beat song in the "do-wah" idiom. Complex arrangements with harps and violins accompanied Flo's clear, blues-jazz style of vocal embellishments, foreshadowing the "Supreme" sound by three years. This did not fit in with Gordy's plan for The Supremes' first big record. When The Supremes came to Motown, it had been made clear that Diane Ross would sing lead on most songs. As Mary put it, "Well, it was pretty well established when we went to Motown that Diana would be the lead singer. Prior to that the three of us had shared the lead — but it was agreed upon. Yes, it was kind of hard to get used to..." Gordy decided that Diane's voice had more commercial value and the young girls wanted the group to succeed. As Mary Wilson explained, "It was an adult attempt to say, 'Ok, if this is the way it's going to be, fine.'" Because they were in a group, she felt the background voices were just as important as the lead.

In August 1962, The Supremes' third release, "Your Heart Belongs To Me," another Smokey Robinson production, made the *Billboard* chart for three weeks, peaking at 95. Mary talked about The Supremes' activities between 1961 and 1964: "We were doing basically record hops around Detroit and around 1963-64 we started tours with The Dick Clark Tour but we also toured with Motown tours which were successful and we went to Florida and places like that. But, basically, we stayed close around Detroit." The group was given an opportunity to travel in the "MotorTown Revue." This three month tour through the South and concluding at New York's Apollo Theatre was The Supremes' first trip out of Detroit. "The only time we had trouble was in Alabama. We used to take turns asking whether we could use bathrooms in filling stations. Once a man started shooting a shotgun at us when we were all foolish enough to get out of our bus," Flo recalled.

The tour was followed by another record late that summer. "Let Me Go The Right Way" climbed to 90 during six weeks on *Billboard.* Undaunted by the lack of a hit record, The Supremes continued to refine their stage technique by attending the Artist Development Program, practicing in the studios with other groups, and appearing at Detroit clubs. At one time, Flo filled in for one of The Marvelettes on tour. Although The Supremes could not get a winning record, they built a reputation of being sophisticated young women which impressed Gordy; The Supremes had the drive for showmanship making them Gordy's favorites within the company.

Mary Wilson described the relationship: "First of all, I would think we were very special to Berry. We were sort of like his pets...he liked us very much as young girls...special to him. I would say out of everyone there we had a unique and special relationship with Berry—being girls. I personally had a very fun relationship with Berry. We did a lot of growing up together . We learned how to play chess together— things like that." The Supremes had five unsatisfactory record releases in two years which Flo described as "depressing." Smokey Robinson's attempts to recreate his production achievements for The Supremes failed.

While The Supremes were experiencing failure, Martha and the Vandellas' second record was on the *Billboard* charts for sixteen weeks, peaking at 29. The Vandellas and The Supremes had different producers. Martha and the Vandellas' "Come and Get These Memories" was the first team production of Eddie Holland, Lamont Dozier, and Brian Holland. The Vandellas' second hit with this winning production team was more triumphant. "Heatwave" climbed to Number 4 with fourteen weeks on *Billboard.* These Holland-Dozier-Holland productions for Martha and the Vandellas indicated to Gordy a hit song for The Supremes might be realized.

The Supremes' first recording for Holland-Dozier-Holland was "When The Lovelight Starts Shining Through His Eyes." The Supremes finally had a hit in the top-forty. This song peaked at Number 23 for a total of eleven weeks on *Billboard* in November, 1963. The turning point for Ross, Ballard, and Wilson was the following spring.

At the time that Holland-Dozier-Holland began working with The Supremes, Martha and the Vandellas continued their accomplishments with different producers. The Vandellas' "Dancing in the Streets," written and produced by Mickey Stevenson, reached Number 2. This song was more adult oriented while it maintained a strong teen-age dance beat.   Martha Reeves outlined the events leading to this song's production: "This was a very bad time all over the United States.   We were just starting to have different confusions in different cities, riots and what have you. I think the writers were inspired mainly because of this, to try an effort to get people to dance and be happy instead of the riots."

The Supremes wanted an impressive record after three struggling years with Motown while The Marvelettes, Mary Wells, and Martha and the Vandellas recorded hit records. Holland-Dozier-Holland positively changed the direction of The Supremes' career with "When the Lovelight Starts Shining Through His Eyes." These producers developed a musical style befitting Diane Ross's unique vocals. Mary Wilson recalled: "We always felt they were giving us sort of teeny-bop songs like 'Where Did Our Love Go?' We didn't want to record that at all. They said, 'Trust us, it'll be a hit.' We said, 'Yes, but it sounds like a kid song. It's not like Martha and the Vandellas' 'Dancing in The Streets.' It's 'Baby, Baby,' Very childish right? Eddie said, 'Just trust us, it's going to be a hit.' I was the main one saying we'll do it, but my god. It was one of our biggest hits."

Childish or not, "Where Did Our Love Go?" was the first of seven consecutive Number-One million selling Supremes' singles produced by Holland-Dozier-Holland. The teeny-bop delivery of Diane Ross was further emphasized in her personal appearance. Her slight build and wide eyes complemented her baby-doll voice with an overall teasing seductiveness. Unlike Martha Reeves who had a variety of vocal stylings, vocal training, and an independent attitude, The Supremes' lead singer had a style and attitude which Gordy, as mentor, could develop.

Motown's biggest sales year to date was 1964 and with Mary Wells' recording of "My Guy;" she became Motown's first superstar. Mary Wells' recordings helped to establish Motown as a nationally recognized recording company. At the age of 21, Mary Wells had a national following and big dreams. Twentieth Century-Fox offered her what appeared to be a better recording contract than Gordy's. She left Motown in 1964, but never had another hit record. Gordy was determined not to lose anymore of his artists after making them stars. The loss of Wells and the rising popularity of The Supremes allowed Gordy to focus attention on Diane Ross as Wells' heir-apparent.

Chapter IV

"Where Did Our Love Go?" remained Number-one for four weeks for a total of fourteen weeks on *Billboard*. In the studio, this song was a disappointment for the producers as well as The Supremes. This song had a different sound and rhythm than their previous works and because of this, the producers were not sure how to approach it. Lyricist Eddie Holland was not satisfied with Diane's lead vocal and preferred Mary's softer voice on the lead. With the song's outcome in doubt, he discussed changing the lead vocal with "the girls" as they were called. However, Lamont Dozier convinced Eddie Holland to listen to the track again; Diane's vocal remained. The subsequent success of "Where Did Our Love Go?" assured her position as the star Supreme after three years and nine flops with Motown. An album, WHERE DID OUR LOVE GO, was marketed to capture the sales momentum of that single and the following Number-one singles, "Baby Love" and "Come See About Me." Motown also released MEET THE SUPREMES, an album of those earlier TAMLA singles to capture the sales demand of the group's "overnight" success.

During the summer, The Supremes began a series of personal appearances nationwide beginning with the Dick Clark "Cavalcade of Stars" tour of the United States. Motown had to convince Clark to accept The Supremes for the tour. Although the group was not well known at the beginning of the tour, the popularity of "Where Did Our Love Go?" proved correct this decision to include The Supremes on the tour. The Cavalcade was recorded in The Santa Monica Civic Auditorium in August for later performances on closed circuit television in theatres under the title of the Teenage Music International Show, the TAMI Show. At this time, Diane Ross became known as the more sophisticated "Diana Ross." When the tour ended, the trio returned to Detroit to record and sign a second set of contracts with Motown.

Motown artists were under two contracts with the company. The recording contracts were made between the artist and the Motown Record Corporation; the management contracts were made with Motown's subsidiary, I.T.M.I. The Supremes signed both of these three year contracts on August 10, 1964.

The Motown policy of releasing a restricted number of recordings was guaranteed by the recording contract. Motown could record as many songs by an artist as it desired, but the contract did not require a minimum number of releases for the artist. Another Motown practice was to discourage the artists from seeking outside legal counsel when signing contracts. The company acted as both the employer and legal agent in these business procedures. Trusting in the good faith of the company and encouraged by the success of "Where Did Our Love Go?," The Supremes entered into three year exclusive contracts with the companies.

Recording contracts and management agreements vary from company to company. The American Federation of Musicians has published a standard agreement which details the basic functions of a recording contract. The Second Recording Agreement between Motown and Florence Ballard is compared herein.

Standard recording agreements were generally made for a term of one year with provisions for four additional option periods of one year each. The company was not bound to extend the original one year period. In the event an artist was unable to fulfill the minimum requirement to record, the company could extend the term of the contract equal to the length of the artist's delinquency, or suspend the agreement. The Second Recording Agreement was made with a strict delinquency clause: Motown "shall not be obligated to pay you any sum while you remain in default of any material provision of this agreement."

The royalty to the artist is based on a percentage of the single records sold at the suggested retail price. For new artists, this may be four or five percent. The company will discount ten percent of the sales figures as an adjustment for damaged or returned records. The royalty for an album is a percentage of the cost of the vinyl disc only. The percentage granted an artist is lowered for out-of-country sales due to

additional costs of distribution and rate of exchange. Royalty payments to new artists are low because of the costs incurred in production of previous unsold records.

Royalties become payable after the costs of the production are met. Advance payments made to an artist for the production of unsold records are calculated against the sales of the hit records, if any. Motown paid The Supremes $12.50 for each master recording and a percentage of each record sold. It is doubtful that the production costs for The Supremes' previous nine releases were calculated into the royalty of "Where Did Our Love Go?" In a 1966 Motown meeting agenda, cost analysis was discussed. The song in question was Jimmy Ruffin's hit single "What Becomes of the Broken Hearted." *"It is a hit, who cares? But is it really a hit after costs? Devise a method for figuring out how much it costs."* Artists are paid union scale for the recording sessions, unless other arrangements are negotiated, until all the costs are recouped. Recording expenses vary from several thousand dollars for a single to upwards of $50,000 for an album. Motown had one advantage over larger companies because it was small and had its own studios. Bateman recalls the production process: "I think [with] most of the things we cut it and we cut it until—I was also an engineer there, before producing—anyway, we cut it until we felt it was perfect. Generally, we'd cut it and listen to it and listen to it again, and if we didn't like it we'd cut it again. You know, it wasn't a thing, we might cut on a side all day and all day the next day." Albums which contain previously released material are less expensive. Motown albums usually contained at least one hit single. The royalty Motown paid The Supremes was divided evenly among Ross, Wilson, and Ballard. The corporation set these earnings aside in a trust and paid the trio an allowance which increased from $50 weekly in 1964 to $225 in 1967. "We really don't know where all our money is. We just trust our advisors and they take care of it for us," Diana told an interviewer in 1966. Florence explained in a 1975 interview, "We received an allowance of $225 dollars a week and the other money was supposedly put into savings accounts, stocks, bonds...."

A record company is generally obligated to pay royalties to the featured artist, not session musicians. The number of sides recorded during the term of each option period varies with each period. The company reserves the exclusive rights to choose which songs are released. In other words, the artist may record six sides for three singles, but the company may elect to shelve the masters. In addition to full ownership of the masters, the company may have full rights to a group name. The company will seek to prevent the use of that name by any member who leaves the group. In situations without this exclusivity clause, individuals of the original group formed new alliances with the same name. Motown retained the right to the name "Supremes" in the contracts. According to the Motown contracts, Ross, Wilson, and Ballard had no interest or right of ownership of the group name. Paragraph 15, section A of the Second Recording Agreement states: "The collective name of the group is 'The Supremes.' We shall have all the same right in the collective name that we have to use your name pursuant to paragraph 6 [Promotion] and you shall not use the group name except subject to the restrictions set forth in that paragraph. In the event you withdraw from the group, or for any reason cease to participate in its live or recorded performances, you shall have no further right to use the group name for any purpose."

Motown also reserved the right to substitute members within the group, royalties would be only on recordings by the artist, not those made by the substitute. Furthermore, recordings leased or transferred to other agents would become the company's royalty, not the artist's. The Second Recording Agreement stated that Motown was not obligated to make any recordings, exploit any, or exploit any service of the artist.

The contracts with nightclubs, television networks, and other public appearances were negotiated through I.T.M.I. Again, Florence Ballard: "I didn't receive any royalty statements and I never saw any contracts that we had for different clubs, just the recording contracts, but there are other contracts that are negotiated to perform in a nightclub." The artists did not involve themselves in these arrangements.

Through I.T.M.I., income from these appearances was also placed in the fund in the joint name of Motown and the artist.

At the time The Supremes signed the extension on their contracts, Motown was making entertainment history as the country's leading black record company; The Supremes were sharing this achievement with The Temptations, Four Tops, Martha and the Vandellas, and Stevie Wonder. Gordy claimed that a single Supremes' record would automatically sell half a million copies upon release. Aggressive promotion by a record company can make the difference between fame or failure. Mike Klenfner of Arista Records' promotion division describes record promotion as the job of creating excitement to sell the product. There are three levels of promotion: the local representative who works with radio, newspaper and stores; the regional representative who manages several local offices; and the main office which directs the entire company promotion program. Independent promoters represent several companies in markets without company branch offices.

The promoter's goal is to get the product on radio station playlists. Repeated air play generates public awareness of the artist and the record. This exposure increases the sales potential. It is to the artist's advantage to visit stations to meet disc jockeys and program directors. Public contact by way of visiting stores, press interviews, school and hospital appearances can establish the artist in a given market. It takes a cooperative artist and an organized promoter to make this work well. Within large record companies, demands for the services of the promotion department can become critical. Because of the limits of personnel, a company may not cultivate one artist or record in favor of another. An artist may hire an independent promoter if the company cannot give the needed assistance to advance a career.

When Mary Wells left Motown for Twentieth Century-Fox, her public relations agent with Motown, Al Abrams, began working for The Supremes. The tour of The Supremes on the Cavalcade was an important promotional device. Frank Barsalona, founder of Premier Talent, stated that Clark paid little for the acts, and was a tough negotiator. A record company represented on a Clark production almost guaranteed radio exposure, benefitting both the company and the artist.

Through Motown's efforts of developing and promoting their acts, the group was seen publicly unlike many girl-groups of the day who were primarily studio singers. After the initial exposure on the Cavalcade, The Supremes embarked on a series of personal appearances. "That's when we started doin' the hard work--meeting disc jockeys, interviews, charm school, bein' nice to build ourselves up to pay the bills," recalled Diane for *Look* magazine. The Supremes began 1965 as the headline act of the "MotorTown Revue" in Detroit; the tour ended in Europe. After appearing in London, Paris, and Brussels, The Supremes went to Los Angeles to film a guest appearance in a beach party movie.

The wonderful reputation of The Supremes grew with each exposure. Motown booked the trio into nighclubs across the country. The Supremes appeared at The Clay House Inn, Bermuda; Blinstrubs, Boston; The Safari Room, San Jose; The Twin Coaches, Pittsburgh. The most important club date came in July, 1965 when The Supremes opened at the Copacabana in New York City. This engagement was reviewed in *Time*, and praised by prominent entertainment figures. Motown even released an album of the event, LIVE AT THE COPA; Sammy Davis, Jr. wrote the liner notes. Although Florence's solo was not included in the album, her comedy lines remained. On the opening of "You're Nobody 'Til Somebody Loves You," Diane sings, "You may be rich, you may possess the world and all its gold, but gold won't bring you happiness when you're growing old," Flo interrupts with "Now wait a minute honey, I'm not so sure about that!" The Supremes had made the big-time.

Special appearances of the Supremes on television were scheduled between tours. They were guests of Ed Sullivan three times and sang on "Shindig", "Hullabaloo", and "Hollywood Palace". They were television guests of Red Skelton, Steve Allen, and Dean Martin. The Supremes celebrated the opening of the Houston Astrodome with Judy Garland. They even gave a concert in Philharmonic Hall at Lincoln Center.

The million selling gold records continued to spin in 1965 with three more Number-one singles: "Stop! In the Name of Love," "Back in My Arms Again," and "I Hear A Symphony." Another album, MORE HITS, was marketed to seize the sales momentum created by these singles. The public identification of each Supreme became more evident in mid-1965. The cover of MORE HITS featured each girl with her own autograph across the front of individual photographs. The lyrics of "Back in My Arms Again" made direct references to The Supremes, "How can Mary tell me what to do?" and "Flo, she don't know". Teenage America quickly learned who Flo and Mary were, and mimiced their distinctive choreography for "Stop! In the Name of Love" with thrust hands out in front like a traffic cop.

Motown also released a series of five specialty albums: MERRY CHRISTMAS, LIVE AT THE COPA, WE REMEMBER SAM COOKE, A BIT OF LIVERPOOL, COUNTRY WESTERN & POP. These albums were a clear example of Gordy's determination to broaden The Supremes' audience, making them more than just teen music hit makers. The producers for these albums had an opportunity to experiment with a different 'Supreme' sound. On the country album, each Supreme sang lead on Willie Nelson's "It Makes No Difference Now." Florence delivered a belting performance of the classic, "Ain't That Good News" on the Sam Cooke album. Their newest records sold automatically and crossed over black and white radio playlists.

The constant travel and recording schedule necessary to keep The Supremes in the public light was physically exhausting. Before the Copa opening, Florence, due to illness, could only rehearse for one week of the month long rehearsal. When asked how the group spent spare time on tour she replied, "When you get off work, you just want to go to bed." During the date at Blinstrub's, Diane nearly collapsed on stage; Gordy gave the trio time to rest. Mary remarked that the strain of singing lead was taking a toll on Diane and felt the responsibility for singing should be divided evenly among the trio.

The demands of their career placed restrictions on their

personal lives. Since their first hit record in the summer of 1964, The Supremes had only one or two weeks off during the next two years. They had to combine a social life into their performance schedule. In a 1966 interview, Diane mentioned the group went to the nightclub Arthur with their driver and Motown associates. "It's not that we've forgotten about men, said Diane, "We just realize that right now work, really hard work, has got to be the most important thing in our lives so dating has got to come second." Florence added, "And since we're on the road a lot there's really no time to get too serious with any one guy. Besides, we're all young and we want to see the world before we settle down." Diane teased that Florence would be the first to get married. In 1966, Florence began dating Berry Gordy's driver, Tommy Chapman.

Mary Wilson commented on the life of a Supreme: "It was so fascinating to be doing what we were doing that we combined our social life and singing and about being so thrilled about the whole thing. I think—I don't think we missed anything. It really was [exhausting], but that, too, was something I enjoyed. It was rough on a lot of people because of the schedule. Flying at night to get into London or wherever to do an interview and right to the show. The constant movement can be very hard on a person if the person does not really enjoy traveling or doing that sort of thing." The Supremes were opening doors for other black entertainers; their accomplishments were not created out of luck, but determination and hard work by them and the Motown organization. "You do get tired, but it's fair", commented Diane.

Television dates became more frequent in 1966 after an initial disappointment on the "Ed Sullivan Show" when they were rushed on and off stage. During this time, through the constant exposure, it became evident Diana Ross was more assertive than her partners. In the *Look* interview her drive to master every facet of entertainment came through with a certain hard edge. "On 'Hullabaloo,' they gave me a cue card with a stupid speech on it to say. How dare they do that? I could be the mistress of ceremonies, but they never ask me.

On the evening of June 8, 1987, Alan White hosted the opening
of an exhibit entitled "Forever Faithful: A Tribute to
Florence Ballard of the Supremes" at the Whiteley Gallery in
Los Angeles. The VIP guest of this very special evening was
Miss Lisa Chapman, Flo's youngest daughter.

Florence Ballard is remembered by Mary Wilson
in a specially commissioned painting by artist
Ted Le Master. [Whiteley Gallery photo, Randall
Wilson Collection]

Mary Wilson and Lisa Chapman pose together at
the Whiteley Gallery Exhibit opening of
"Forever Faithful. A Tribute to Florence Ballard"

Lisa Chapman   with   Randall Wilson
at the Whiteley Gallery in L. A. on June 8,
1987. [photo courtesy of Thomas Ingrassia]

Mary Wilson not only contributed many personal items to the exhibit,
but commissioned a special video tribute to Florence. The rare video
concluded with photos of Florence as she sang "The Impossible Dream"
from her ABC album.

A contemplative Florence (l) during a European photo session and below, Mary, Florence and Diana pose as the internationally known Supremes. (Courtesy of Frans de Beer, Holland)

Motown kept The Supremes image before the public as displayed in this radio promotion ad and sheet music. Below, Florence poses front and center from this European promotion photo. (Courtesy of Thomas Ingrassia and John Culver)

August 29, 1967, (above left) Florence welcomed fan Alice Manica into her home. Above right, Florence in Europe. Florence Ballard looking back on The Supremes in 1975. (Courtesy of Thomas Ingrassia and John Culver)

May 7, 1967, Florence Ballard made her final appearance on the **Ed Sullivan Show**. Above (l-r) Florence, Diana and Mary perform "Mame" and below (l-r) Florence, Mary and Diana sing "Second Hand Rose" in the "Thoroughly Modern Millie" production number. (Randall Wilson Collection)

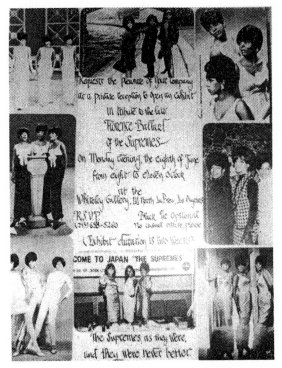

One of many photo collages on display at the
Los Angeles exhibit tribute to Florence Ballard,
June 8, 1987. [Randall Wilson Collection]

Florence Ballard was the featured personality in the October 20, 1968 issue of "Detroit." [Randall Wilson Collection]

The record sleeve of "Love Ain't Love" [Randall Wilson Collection]

I see all the phonies who never had one number one hit running around actin' like big stars. I've got something they don't have, and the kids know. I'm for real."

What Miss Ross had was the support of Berry Gordy while the group was drifting apart off stage. As early as January, 1966, during a hometown engagement at Detroit's Roostertail, the press was speculating: when would Diane leave the trio for a solo career? She maintained that all decisions were made by Gordy. "It's up to Berry. I—we—do what he says," she told *Detroit Free Press* writer Mort Persky during the interview before Flo and Mary arrived. Mary talked about the Gordy/Supremes connection: "Each relationship was different. How can I say that—Diana and Berry had a very different relationship and it had a lot to do with the career of the group. I would say that was their common bond — only my opinion— you'll have to ask her. He and Florence did not have the same type of close relationship that Berry and Diana or Berry and I had. I would say Diana was more special to him...."

The Supremes' homecoming at The Roostertail on the Detroit River was handled like a Broadway show. WXYZ radio aired the performance and interviewed the trio on the "Lee Allen Show". WXYZ reviewer Dick Osgoode rated The Supremes' opening as among the five great performances of his life. In performance The Supremes were harmonious. The *Free Press* review was glowing with superlatives. Their handling of ballads and standard songs was praised above their own material. "They were at their best with finely emotional interpretations of 'People' and 'A Place for Us.'" When Diana Ross introduced Flo Ballard as "the quiet one," she replied with dead-pan comic timing, "that's what you think." Ken Barnard wrote that with Flo's one-liners drawing laughter, the group did not need special stage material written. Indeed, while critics called Diana Ross a new Eartha Kitt, Flo was being hailed as a young Pearl Bailey.

On stage, Florence Ballard added a classy softness to the act with her natural flair for comedy and smooth vocals according to their manager Thomas Bowles. Remarking on The Supreme sound, Florence proudly told "That's where our real talent comes in, when they give us a song, it's up to us to work with it and put something of ourselves into it." Florence's controlled mezzo-soprano can be heard underscoring Diana Ross's lead vocal on many of The Supremes early songs especially "You Keep Me Hanging On."

Regarding her own singing Flo commented, "I had a music teacher who wanted me to sing what she felt was really good music, like Handel or 'Ave Maria'." In the *Look* interview, she talked about her capabilities. "None of us can read music, but I think I could be an opera singer if I could only have more training." Abraham Silver, one of Flo's high school teachers, confirmed her opinion. Florence and Mary both learned Bach, Beethoven, and Mozart in school. Flo Ballard was promoted two years ahead of her class in a special music program. Silver told the *Washington Post*, "With that background, their voices could adapt to every style. Florence had a big proper voice. She stood out early."

During a rehearsal with many Motown artists in attendance at the Twenty Grand, Gordy dropped Flo's only solo, "People," from the act and gave it to Diane. Of course this came as a bitter disappointment to the Quiet Supreme. This was not the first song taken from her and given to Diane. Flo was originally slated to sing "The House of The Rising Sun" on the A BIT OF LIVERPOOL album. Mary noted that Flo was able to take things in stride, lovable, but was misunderstood. For Florence it also marked the beginning erosion in her relationship with the Motown boss. As the record and public acclaim endured, Florence Ballard and Mary Wilson were frustratingly relegated to the background, unable to prove their individual talents as singer. The shared microphone of The Supremes was gone.

The Motown production system of using prerecorded tracks was firmly in place when The Supremes were touring full time. Diana Ross recorded the lead vocals separately; at times anonymous background voices were substituted in the recordings. Florence and Mary would have to learn the songs afterward for performances. Looking back on those days, Mary commented: "In the early days we would sing right along with the band. And that was really a thrill, however, as things got more hectic later and we had to tour, the producers

Flo taking lead on "People"
(l-r) Mary Wilson, Florence Ballard, Diana Ross

35

wanted all the material ready and recorded so that when we came to town we could hop right in and record."

The list of top-ten songs increased in 1966 with: "My World Is Empty Without You", "Love is Like an Itching in My Heart," and "You Can't Hurry Love." The album I HEAR A SYMPHONY contained a few standards as well as the Holland-Dozier-Holland compositions. "With a Song in My Heart" by Rodgers and Hart was included to introduce this more young adult side of The Supremes' appeal in an album of hit singles.

The album SUPREMES A GO GO followed in the summer of 1966 with Mary Wilson featured on a re-do copy of The Vandellas' "Come and Get These Memories." Although Florence had not been featured in any album package after 1964, her performance of Sam Cooke's "Ain't That Good News" was cited as a "noteworthy success" by Persky. Mary and Florence were never featured on a single release.

The Supremes pose for a record jacket cover while on tour in Europe, 1965.
(l-r) Diana Ross, Mary Wilson, Florence Ballard.

[photo courtesy of Thomas Ingrassia]

Chapter V

The Supremes matured into top rated entertainers bringing to Motown acceptance in the established music business. Their very success also created a force within the company that changed its future. The Supremes had become a top-of-the-line entertainment product. The management of the group, and the other successful groups at Motown, had to mature as well if Gordy's dream-machine was to continue its achievements. The Supremes trip to Britain in the winter of 1966 was discussed in a company note, *"Supremes need intelligent road managers."* Motown began licensing the popular Supremes name to a brand of bread from which the company received a tenth of a cent royalty on each sale. Problems of balancing a career with a personal life were again putting a strain on the group during this time, although rumors of internal fights among The Supremes were largely discounted by the company.

Gordy reportedly settled whatever problems were developing within the trio for a time in the spring after their European tour. He recounted his efforts to loosen up on career demands in an interview in the fall of 1966. He felt that the group was more sensible about life and relaxed about their love lives. "It is always the little things that blow-up. If the little things can be cleared up before they get big, trouble can be prevented." Gordy did not know, or tell, what direction the group might take, but Motown was preparing to enlarge its operations beyond the houses on West Grand Boulevard. The Motown family had adopted a mid-level management structure to oversee the day-to-day operations and separate the artists from the top administration.

Billboard announced in mid-1966 that Motown was planning to open operating facilities on the West Coast; the Los Angeles operations would be for videotape and film production. CKLW-TV in Windsor, Ontario, Canada, was Motown's source for local productions at this time. Television specials for The Supremes were planned as a part of this expanded operation. The future plans for the company were set in motion during the summer. During the last part of the year and continuing through 1967, changes and pressures began anew for The Supremes. Abrams was fired as the Motown publicity director and a clamp was placed on the group's accessibility in order to preserve their public image.

"We feel a great sense of responsibility toward the kids that buy our records. It's like we know that they are watching us all the time and following everything we do. We'd feel terrible letting them down by acting in a way that would cause them to lose respect for us. We've never been known as goody-goody girls because that's not real, but we've always been very conscious about the way we carry ourselves and the people we associate with. So many kids get caught up in a life of dope and crime and that's bad. We've tried to stay away from that sort of thing and now with so many people looking to us as examples, we feel even more strongly about it," stated Diana in a press interview. As for education, Florence advised, "Too many kids seem to think that they're wasting time staying in school. Nothing could be further from the truth. Whatever a person wants to be, the better his education is the better his chances will be for success. This is true in show business as in any other job."

Florence Ballard was being squeezed out of the trio at the end of 1966. The constant traveling and personal conflicts were affecting morale of the group. Flo did not have a close relationship with Gordy. Their rift, which began after her solo number was dropped from the act, continued growing. She was still dating Gordy's driver and in her own way began acting out her frustrations by being late for rehearsals and interviews. In New Orleans Florence had been up all night drinking and according to Mary, Diane and Mary were left to sing duets together on stage. Although she was nick-named "the quiet one," Richard Lingeman of The *New York Times* observed that Flo could be "outspoken in an abrupt, flaunting way if the spirit moves her." In 1970, Flo told *Michigan Chronicle* writer Rita Griffin, "I think that dialogue [quiet one] was written into the act as a hint, because if anything, I was outspoken. If something didn't appear right, I would mention it. It's just that people know where to hit me." She was criticized for gaining weight, performing below standards, drinking, and for quitiing high school [contrary to the Motown press release].

In a tightly controlled organization such as Motown, outspokenness was not a virtue. Martha Reeves also made suggestions to Gordy which were met with his hostility. According to Reeves, Gordy told her not to try to run his company. "I retaliate," she said, "where other people would be quiet. I speak." After 1967, Martha and the Vandellas did not have a hit record. For Flo Ballard, the consequences of being outspoken would be more disastrous.

The Supremes were appearing more frequently in fashionable nightclubs. The act now emphasized standards as their own hits were condensed into medleys. Vocally, Diana Ross carried the entire show although Flo's comedy lines were retained. Even on television the group moved away from performing their own material and concentrated on Tin Pan Alley and Broadway standards. They appeared on a television special featuring Rodgers and Hart music in the spring 1967. Gordy produced an album SUPREMES SING RODGERS AND HART, as a Motown version of Ella Fitzgerald's classic Rodgers and Hart Songbook, with notes by Gene Kelly. Mary Wilson was featured on "Falling In Love With Love;" Diana Ross got all other leads and one solo. The record was originally planned to be a double album including the charming "Manhattan" as a shared lead of Florence and Diane. This tune was released in a special package of unreleased material in 1986.

During the spring a meeting with Gordy was held to discuss the future of The Supremes. The prospects of Diana Ross becoming a soloist and Flo Ballard's future as a Supreme were discussed. In 1975 Florence highlighted this meeting for a Detroit reporter that during 1966 she was being encouraged to leave the group. "It was mentioned to me that 'Florence you said that if Diana wanted to be a single artist that you wouldn't stand in her way.' So I said, 'That's exactly what I said, but I didn't say I would leave the group.' And after that it kept going on and on, 'Florence you're a millionaire and you're just twenty-four years old and you can retire any time you want.' So, I got the feeling that I wasn't wanted...."

Twice in the winter of 1967, Flo missed public performances due to illness. When it became evident that Flo would miss another performance [a benefit by Motown for a black education fund, a favorite Motown charity] on a shared bill with the Buffalo Springfield, Fifth Dimension, and Johnny Rivers at the Hollywood Bowl on April 30, 1967, Motown arranged for a substitute to appear with Mary and Diane. Cindy Birdsong, a member of the Philadelphia girl-group Patti LaBelle and the Bluebells, replaced Flo. Cindy Birdsong knew The Supremes professionally from the early "MotorTown Revues." Even in those years people commented on how similar Flo and Cindy looked. Cindy had been called to Detroit by Larry Maxwell to rehearse with Mary Wilson the evening before the concert. Cindy Birdsong filled in so well most fans did not know Florence Ballard was missing. The *Los Angeles Times* reviewed Cindy Birdsong as a "strong sub...blending effectively."

Florence Ballard was well enough to perform with Diana Ross and Mary Wilson the following week in a return engagement at the Copacabana. *Variety* called the act "polished to a high gloss" with "nifty" stage business. On the "Tonight Show" Diane acknowledged that a stand-in was available for Florence and Mary, not herself, when Carson asked them about the hectic schedule they maintained. Their next club date, June 13 to June 23, was a debut at the Cocoanut Grove in Los Angeles. Again the reviews were excellent. This was a "bombastic" show with Diana Ross standing out vocally; Florence and Mary were important "mainstays." The trio was one of "obvious talent" with beautiful counterpoint harmony. Aside from the missed performances earlier in the year, the internal criticism that Florence Ballard was not performing to standards did not occur in any press reviews. Florence denied that she was leaving the group in a June interview in *Soul.* The two nightclub bookings were immediately before the July Las Vegas engagement at the Flamingo.

The Supremes' second stay at the Flamingo was better reviewed than their first the previous October. The *Variety* review again was matchless; Ross, Wilson, and Ballard had a "superb, distinctive blend." As Las Vegas is considered an influential entertainment center, this appearance was of particular importance to Gordy and The Supremes. The program that had been discussed earlier was to take place during this two week commitment. The booking was extended for a third week and the trio's name was changed to "Diana Ross and the Supremes." Concurrently, their new single "Reflections" was released with the same billing. This change ended nearly two years of speculation by the press whether Diana Ross would remain with The Supremes or become a soloist; she was able to do both. Another important change occurred to further propel Miss Ross as the group's star. The details of the off stage events are not verified, but the results are well known.

Cindy Birdsong was called to Las Vegas to view the show for a few nights. "I had to go watch the show and I felt I was making her [Flo] uneasy," Cindy told the *Detroit Free Press.* Whether Florence Ballard knew Cindy Birdsong was in Las Vegas is disputable. *Jet Magazine* described a "hair-pulling, knock-down-drag-out fight over the change in billing." During a performance Flo cut up on stage and during her line "thin may be in but fat is where it's at," she turned her bulging middrift to the audience. Flo's account indicated that Motown officials prevented her from returning to the stage, that Gordy would throw her off if she tried. Cindy Birdsong changed into Flo Ballard's costume and went on instead. Motown publicity said the situation was temporary; Flo Ballard was exhausted from the schedule. Gordy is quoted as saying Flo "who has been in and out of the group over the past five years because of her personal problems, which she hopes to work out," will be substituted by Cindy Birdsong. In court testimony later, the Motown lawyer said it was because of her behavior. Whatever the reason, her unwillingness to continue in the background without recognition, conflicts with Gordy and Diana Ross on the handling of the group, the change was made. A stunned Flo Ballard flew home to a shell-shocked Detroit torn by race riots near the very neighborhoods where The Supremes bought their fami-

41

lies' homes. While the smoke cleared over the city, Florence entered Henry Ford Hospital for a short rest.

The press release continued: "Florence Ballard is not currently appearing with The Supremes, but the absence is not because of Diana's billing as a star." The following week Motown vice-president Michael Roshkind met Florence Ballard at the Northland Inn in a meeting which was just the beginning of the difficulties Florence Ballard faced for the next eight years of her life.

The explanation of Flo's departure from The Supremes remained elusive for three years. When Diana Ross and the Supremes sang at the Michigan State Fair in Detroit one month after Flo was replaced, Miss Ross told the *Detroit News*, "We're still good friends," she paused, "We always had to give Florence a little pull, a little push...," and stopped. Mary Wilson added, "We all understand. It's hard work traveling around all the time." Later in the interview Diane and Mary explained they had given Motown an ultimatum for more time off, one month every six months or two weeks every three months. Not until 1970 when Florence Ballard filed an $8.5 million lawsuit against Gordy, Ross and Motown, did the public begin to ascertain how her dismissal was handled.

On July 26, 1967 when Flo Ballard met with Roshkind at which time the decision of Berry Gordy was made clear: Florence Ballard was permanently out of The Supremes. She was offered an extension of her contracts, indicated in the Supplemental Agreement, but withdrew that option. Instead she signed an agreement that offered her a six year annual gratuity of $2,500, a total of $15,000. The Supplemental Agreement stated that she was not allowed to identify herself as having been a member of The Supremes, nor would she receive any future royalties from Motown. As in previous contract negotiations, Flo Ballard had no legal representation during this meeting. The contract was signed by Ballard and Motown executives. The Quiet Supreme left the meeting in tears but determined to receive a more equitable settlement from the corporation.

Florence Ballard retained the law firm of Baun, Okrent and Vulpe on August 24, 1967 for a 20% retainer against Berry Gordy Enterprises and Motown Records from January 15, 1961 [when she signed with the company] through 1967. Leonard Baun first met Flo in July and she signed with him in August. The meeting had been arranged through a referral by Hank Warren. Leonard Baun was retained to act as her advisor, business manager, and attorney. Ironically this was one week before Diana Ross and the Supremes appeared in their hometown at the Michigan State Fair with Cindy Birdsong appearing in Flo's place. Everything seemed the same, the trio swirled in pink flowing gowns, the Jimmy Wilkins Band played the familiar Supremes' tunes; however, one song, "Back in My Arms Again," was dropped and never performed again. Cindy later recalled that it was one of the hardest, and yet heartwarming performances for her. Florence brought her family to the show and sat in the front row while the hometown crowd accepted Cindy as "The New" Supreme.

On September 15, 1967 Motown turned over $75,689.00 to Florence through attorney Leonard Baun. This money did not represent a settlement with Motown, but was her joint account with Motown at the Bank of the Commonwealth. At this time Baun induced Florence to create Talent Management with himself as the treasurer and president. As treasurer, he issued $5,000.00 of her money for Talent Management stock to himself.

The proceeding against Motown continued through the fall and on December 5, 1967, Motown released stock possessions in Flo's name to Baun. At this time and using his home address, Baun applied for credit cards in the name of Florence Ballard, Thomas Chapman and himself. $10,003.39 of the trust fund was used to buy 341 shares of diversified growth stock and 343 shares of Dreyfus funds in Flo's name. In 1968, Baun paid himself $43,050.24 in attorney fees.

During the span of time from August, 1967 and February, 1968, Berry Gordy did not meet, or return any of Baun's calls regarding Flo's status with the company. Instead Baun worked with Motown attorney Ralph Seltzer. The two had known each other years before when Baun worked for the firm of Berger, Manson and Keyes in the First National Building in 1953. Seltzer had been the previous occupant in the office. Although acquainted, they had never worked together in any business dealings. The chief negotiator for Motown was George Schiffer, Motown also was represented by the accounts Sydney and Harold Novick. Baun and Schiffer met in Detroit and New York City approximately twelve times. Ralph Jewell, also an attorney, was hired by Baun to assist and William Davis was brought in to help with Flo's income taxes and other financial difficulties. Baun and Jewell met six times to develop ideas on an approach of working with, or through Motown.

Because The Supremes had never been supplied with any documents from Motown, Florence and Baun tried to reconstruct her performance schedule from her passport. Schiffer supplied some of the dates, the few documents were given by Seltzer and Novick. Baun was handicapped by not being familiar with entertainment contracts; therefore, Jewell referred him to a man in New York who was. Jewell met him to devise a method for figuring out Flo's record compensation. From the reconstructed history, Baun and Florence deducted that The Supremes grossed $1.6 million in 1967 out of which hotels, expenses on the road and in the studio were paid. International Talent Management Incorporated, the Motown subsidiary, received 15%. The documentation of these figures in preparation for Flo's case was further clouded by the Motown negotiators. Motown advised Mr. Baun that no contracts for The Supremes existed, or if they did exist, they could not be released. Other contracts with third parties were said to be private and confidential. I.T.M.I. used a booking agency called "Queens" in New York to book their artists. Audits of the books by Baun were referred to Sidney Novick, who was very seldom at the Motown offices. Miss Ballard in the meantime had little money while the settlements were going on. The longer that Motown delayed the less important the audit became, although it was her right by contract to the audit. Motown said it would let Baun audit the books at an expense, but Flo did not have the money for this. She and Baun were led to believe that the amount of her earnings was nowhere near what she had been told. The million dollars had been reduced to thousands after the costs of performances and recordings had been deducted.

The possibility of a lawsuit against Motown was discussed in order to subpoena the documents; however, because Florence wanted to get a single out and get married to Tommy Chapman, the lawsuit idea was dropped in favor of trying to work on a settlement out-of-court. Baun did not feel comfortable with this decision. He thought he would not be able to get a full accounting of the finances without a lawsuit, and that Motown was not "leveling" with him. In the meantime, Davis was preparing Flo's taxes as she had been having problems with the Internal Revenue Service. Until 1965 or 1966, she had not received any royalties and Davis was trying to average back her income for those years. According to Baun all of her earnings were in dispute and therefore covered by his retainer. Florence herself did not know how much money there was, or where any money was. Baun was in constant contact with Motown personnel which were very uncooperative. Baun wrote to Berry Gordy, but Gordy did not reply. Seltzer was incensed that he did this: "They became very upset. When I say, ' they,' Mr. Seltzer became very upset because he thought that I going beyond him or over his head to try to reach Mr. Gordy."

Negotiations continued throughout the fall during which time ABC Records had started making overtures through promoter Lou Zito, who had been with Motown, to get Flo under contract. One agreement with Motown was set to be final and then Seltzer and Novick told Baun it had broken down. Berry Gordy was refusing to go through with it, that he personally would not approve the settlement. The lawsuit was discussed again and again dismissed for a settlement. In order for ABC to sign Florence a complete separation from Motown had to be approved. Motown was not interested in going beyond the original $15,000. "So to speak, they [Motown] treated her as a vassal in my opinion. She worked for them. They controlled her every move, everything she, and Diana Ross and Mary Wilson did, was controlled by Motown, Berry Gordy and International Talent

Management and the people working for them," Baun told in deposition and continued, "Their position was, 'We don't owe you anything. We have paid you for what you've done up to now, that is the end of it.'" Baun advised Florence that the extension agreement of July 26, 1967 was not binding and he advised Motown of the same. The signature was procured without counsel. "These contracts amounted to plain chivalry servitude and we were going to avoid these contracts one way or the other. It didn't enter into my mind one second that I had to go beyond that. I said, 'You are not going to hold her to these contracts, whether you like it or not.' From that moment on our negotiation began to ripen. I told her that the agreements, in my opinion, were not legally binding upon her because of the various factors, moral as well as legal. I felt that Motown took advantage of her or someone in I.T.M.I. took advantage of her." Regrettably Baun took the advice of Jewell, Zito and Motown that sales of The Supremes' records would fall in the future and the determination of their worth was not possible!

"Some records never sell anything. This was borne out later on by virtue of the fact that the records didn't sell that she made as an individual after terminating with Motown," Baun stated, showing his lack of knowledge of the recording industry. As for the monetary interest in The Supremes' name, Baun knew it had a goodwill value, "but to say how much it was worth or how hot it is, I didn't know. I knew it had a value, obviously." Motown, Novick, Seltzer, and Schiffer even denied that Florence had suggested the name for the group.

Finally the General Release agreement was settled. Baun advised Flo that one item deducted from the gross total of The Supremes receipts was for gowns. She told him that they were still in the possession of Motown. 'If they have used your funds or some of your funds, funds that you have one-third interest in to buy personal gowns for you that fit you, I think that you ought to get those gowns or get their present depreciated value.' That is one of the things we used as a criteria and those items of stage apparel that were still in their possession." Baun and Florence settled on a dollar amount, $5,000 from the account of Diana Ross and the Supremes. The nine page settlement was made on February 22, 1968. Baun and Schiffer met in Detroit and according to Baun, Motown settled only to "get this thing over now and avoid future litigation and bitterness between parties." At the Caucus Club after the meeting with Schiffer and Novick, Baun was told, "Take it or leave it. This is it. Take it or forget it, start your lawsuit." The General Release reaffirmed the restrictions on publicity [acknowledgment of having been a Supreme] and royalties from past recordings, and new restrictions on future civil action against Motown, Ross, Wilson, or Birdsong. "One single factor that caused us to enter into the final agreement was the fact that she and Tommy Chapman stressed were very concerned about the fact that she wanted to go into the performing artist field as an individual." Motown did agree to grant a lump sum payment of $160,000 to Ballard. The source of this payment was divided as follows:

Supremes Vocal Group	$20,195.06
Diana Ross and the Supremes	$5,000.00
Motown Record Corporation	$134,809.40

The three checks, representing the trust fund, were sent by Harold Novick to Leonard Baun. Florence Ballard did not receive the money or the associated documents from Motown. Baun was entrusted with $300,000 of Flo's personal assets: "She had, of course, this contract pending with ABC Records for a $15,000 non refundable advance. It was publicly known that Cindy Birdsong had joined the group, that she was not one of The Supremes. It was also discussed on many occasions the fact that Motown was a very powerful factor in the performing artist field, and that they might, if we could not terminate the relationship on a more or less friendly basis, that they might take, in some manner adverse steps to actually impede her career." Baun questioned, "You mean like blackball her?" Mr Baun continued, "To some extent they might have some influence. It was obvious that

Motown did have a lot of influence, that many of the established booking agencies booked for the performing artists who had contracts with Motown, and that they were reluctant, we were told this, in direct conversations. Mr. Zito told me that he had direct conversations with people in New York who felt that they did not, so to speak in their language, want to touch Flo because she was hot, because of what was, more or less, publicly known that friction had developed between Mr. Gordy and Motown's organization. I mentioned this to Miss Ballard. She knew this individual, he was a Jewish man, as I recall, 60 or 70 years old. He was not a young man, but he had been in this field sometime. There was a woman who had a booking agency that was quite knowledgeable. These people both indicated directly in telephone conversations that they had apprehensions in trying to get bookings for Florence. They had received no threats. No one ever told me that, nor did anyone ever say that Motown had gone out of its way to try to impede Miss Ballard's ability to perform as an individual. This was in the back of our minds that they [Motown] might try." Was it discussed with Motown? "Oh, yes, we talked about it naturally. They always laughed it off and said, ' *We wouldn't do anything to harm Florence. She is our friend.*' She was such a friend, we tried to kick her over for $15,000, that sort of thing."

From an early 1968 program *An Evening With Diana Ross and the Supremes.* Florence Ballard's image has been cut out between their Japanese host and Diana Ross at the Tokyo Airport. Berry Gordy and Mary Wilson on the left.

Chapter VI

Florence Ballard was set free from the organization which had guided her to international stardom. As a single artist the responsibility to make the same decisions that Motown had made was hers. At the age of 24, with little experience in business affairs, Flo Ballard was alone in the fast-paced recording industry. A week after the Motown settlement, Thomas Chapman, Gordy's former valet and chauffeur, married Florence Ballard. Tommy Chapman also became his wife's manager for her budding career as a solo artist. Florence did not say much about it. According to one Detroiter, he was not her best choice in this area. Baun described the couple as very much in love in spite of a stormy premarital courtship. Chapman was afraid of quitting Motown, and afraid that Motown might try to cripple Flo's career. "Who was I to disagree?" commented Baun, "I don't think Tommy knew and I don't think that he had the capacity or background to assume the responsibility and the role that he did. I discussed this with his wife on several occasions. They decided this is the way it was going to be." Tommy was young, in his late 20s, and seemingly on the fast-track, quite positive and forthright. It was a delicate decision for Baun to make suggestions.

Lou Zito was the first to contact ABC Records on Flo's behalf before the General Release was completed, he received $3,000 of the $15,000 advance offer of the recording company. Zito told Baun that he had contacted other companies and that ABC was the only one willing to put up the money. Tommy went to New York to work out other deals, but nothing came of it. Baun continued. "We couldn't have very many conversations at all because of the fact that we were afraid this would jeopardize any settlement negotiations with Motown, if they found out that we were negotiating with someone outside their organization before Miss Ballard was legally released from her contract with Motown." The early December Lou Zito deal was reported in a music newspaper as a "nullified" contract because Flo was still under contract with Motown.

ABC Records signed Florence Ballard to a two year exclusive recording contract on March 6, 1968. The record division of the American Broadcasting Corporation had been undergoing a two-year expansion when Ballard went with the company. Their 1966 profits were up 150 percent over the previous year. Dunhill Records along with Trousdale Music, and the New Deal Distribution Network were purchased by ABC Records. The popular vocal groups The Mamas and the Papas and Three Dog Night were on the Dunhill label. In August 1967, ABC picked up the Riverside jazz label. The ABC-Paramount label was changed to 'ABC' in the streamlining of the new expansion. National distribution of the ABC records was managed by a joint venture of four companies, including Twentieth Century-Fox. Not one of the companies was a rhythm and blues or top-forty label.

Although ABC was growing when Flo Ballard signed, it did not have the same concentration of power among black stations and top-forty stations that Motown had built over eight years. Village Voice writer Geoffrey Stokes' case study, *Star Making Machinery*, of rock group Commander Cody and his Lost Planet Airmen, an ABC group, stated that when The Mamas and the Papas broke-up in late 1968, the company's growth was stunted. Moreover, ABC's product distribution was spotty, some branches unprofitable. ABC was not a family organization operating out of seven houses; ABC was looking for an established artist with a 'Supremes' sound with Florence Ballard.

Flo Ballard went to record in the New York studios that spring. The sessions were produced by former Motown producer-writer George Kerr. The only ABC release of these sessions was Kerr's tune "It Doesn't Matter How I Say It." This song had a Motown-style sound with a lyric reminiscent of The Temptations' "The Way You Do The Things You Do." The flip-side was a remake of Little Anthony and the Imperials' "Goin' Out of My Head." In April the single was listed in a two page *Billboard* advertisement of coming ABC products. Because of the conditional release from Motown, ABC could not promote Ballard as a former member of The Supremes.

It is doubtful whether radio programmers knew her name without this tag.

Rosilee Trombley, Music Director of CKLW, the dominant top forty station in Detroit explained how a record is watched in one market to another. " 'Rosilee hit the new Marvin Gaye record.' Well, I check the black sales, I do. When a big record comes in from Detroit by the black radio stations; it happened with this new Marvin Gaye record out there ["Sexual Healing"]. Okay, I know without a doubt, most of the radio stations across the country are saying, ' I wonder what Detroit is going to do with that one.' And Marvin probably has one of the newest, biggest albums of singles out on the street now. But it could have been a handicap for that particular record, if we just sat back and said, 'I don't know,' and not played it right away. And this record company is getting back from the program director in New York or Milwaukee saying, ' how come Detroit is not on that Marvin Gaye record?' Do you understand what I am saying. I do the same thing when you know that various artists have particular roots. I may say, looking at Atlanta, ' I like that Alabama record, but they aren't having any success as a pop record. What am I going to do with it in Detroit?' It is an exchange policy where different markets are responsible for different records and various radio stations." Additional local publicity about Florence was prevented at home because both the *Detroit News* and the *Detroit Free Press* were on strike for nine months. The record went nowhere.

Talent Management, Chapman's company for Flo, hired Al Abrams to handle her publicity. Chapman secured the Joe Glaser agency in New York to arrange nightclub dates. After the first single was released, Flo appeared on a few local television shows on the East Coast, and concert dates with Wilson Pickett, for whom The Primettes had recorded background vocals in 1960. The Sweetheart of America, and toast of two continents, former Supreme Flo Ballard was singing in high school auditoriums. She returned to New York for another series of recording sessions in the summer.

Robert Bateman was brought in at the suggestion of Clarence Avett: "I was doing some work for MGM and he was an accountant there and with most of the major companies you have to wait a few weeks to get your money. I was used to getting mine as soon as I finished what I was doing. I was turned on to him [Otis Smith] by Clarence Avett....I called Otis and told him to get my checks for me. The Supremes were in town at the time and I would treat him to The Supremes at the Copa. That's how our relationship began. He went to work for the Textile Bank in New York. They were the receivers— when you go into bankruptcy, receivership— and he was on the account with them....They sort of turned all that a stuff over to him and they formed Orpheum Production and Otis and I worked together from that and later he moved to another record company and ended up at ABC. He gave me my shot through our past experiences. He said, 'Hey, we've got Florence Ballard over here and I know you worked with her in the past,' and on like that. And that was how it came about."

Bateman produced four sides for Florence. ABC chose "Love Ain't Love," written by Van McCoy, a moving force of the disco sound of the 1970s, for a fall release. Asked if he felt the records were strong enough to be hit records, Bateman replied. "Of course! 'Love Ain't Love' was a Van McCoy song. You are familiar with Van? He is deceased now, but he was a very strong writer, although I am a producer and writer as well, the song itself is the most important thing. I picked that song above— over some of my own because I thought it was strong enough to make it. I have to say I never heard it played either. I knew it was released, because I have a copy of the record. Our turntables are not the ones that make the hits." The flip-side was a Brianbert tune "Forever Faithful" written for Florence by Bateman.

"Love Ain't Love" had a strong driving beat that revealed the power and range of Flo's voice. *Detroit Free Press* writer Barbara Holliday commented, "The Ballard voice? You begin to understand why a trio might split— with two lead singers and only one being featured." "Love Ain't Love" did not make any music charts. Black-oriented radio station WCHB, Detroit, which had supported Motown artists in the early years, placed Ballard's single on its charts, but the other

Detroit stations ignored it. The record was another failure.

ABC Records treated Ballard's records indifferently. *Billboard*'s radio editor Claude Hall does not agree with the theory that a record will sell regardless of air play if it is good. Because of the costs of record production, a major company will only release good records. Moreover, the program director can influence sales, but the criteria used in selection directs the choices. Top-forty playlists are based on record sales, air play in less restrictive markets or on specialized stations. The WABC, New York, playlist is determined by the sales of rhythm and blues records played on WWRL, a black oriented station. A single may sell 30,000 units as a result of exposure on WWRL. Record companies, aware of this, produce for the crossover factor. Russ Regan, president of Twentieth Century-Fox Records and former promoter for Motown, contends that records that failed did not receive proper exposure. When a record was played on air, it sold. For a producer what was considered a "commercial product?" For Robert Bateman how was "commercial" defined? "By listening to the radio....We tried to emulate the other hit records." Again Rosilee Trombley explained: "You have artists that become 'hot', okay, who have served your listeners well, your radio station well, buyers well, okay. People buy the product and you sort of "milk" that. Where we see the demand in sales, see the demand via phone that they hear Elton John. If that is what they want to hear that is what you give them. Until you see a trend, a burnout factor start, where the next record you put on by Elton John isn't as successful as the previous one you played or the ones you played two years ago. Elton just has comeback recently." Even on the special request lines Florence Ballard's singles would not be played. CKLW stated that they did not have the record when it was requested after the *Free Press* article came out in October of 1968.

Flo continued to make some personal engagements in spite of the records' failures. Lou Zito was a second string booking agent for Florence. Although some of his past clients were fairly well known at the time Florence was presumedly being promoted by him, none were in the leagues of The

Supremes, or any of the Motown acts. Zito handled Ruby and the Romantics, who had one hit in 1962, T. Bone Walker, and Big Joe Turner among others. They all grossed under $100,000 in yearly receipts. For his 20% agent fee he only booked her in one show at the Wonder Garden in Atlantic City and one lip-sync show in New York. Tommy Chapman stepped in to try his hand at guiding Flo's career and contacted veteran entertainer Honi Coles who wrote the Chapmans in July 1968: *"I see that according to Lou it is going to be difficult for a short period of time to book Florence through any regular agencies because of her former connection with Motown. I think that you should personally follow up on this and see if this is true by contacting agencies such as William Morrison [sic] and some other top organization in that field."*

Cholly Atkins, Honi Coles' former partner and a Motown choreographer, assisted Florence in putting the Atlantic City show together. Zito complained to Baun that he did not have a product to sell, Flo was not ready, ABC couldn't come up with hits, or she couldn't come up with hits. Baun countered, "I thought Florence had a beautiful voice, the records that I heard her cut. But you know, I was not an expert and I never held myself out to be one and qualified to judge an entertainer's talent. The performance that I heard her perform in Atlantic City left me disappointed. I wouldn't pay to see a performance like that. I thought that she has a beautiful voice. I didn't think she was ready as a single entertainer. She had been improperly coached and had been improperly prepared...I don't think she had proper coaching from a man like Mr. Zito." Baun paid Zito $5,548 between May 7, 1968 and July 29, 1968 without Flo's knowledge. Baun commented, "I don't think in retrospect she should have gone to ABC to cut records. I don't think that ABC had the right concept for her type of singing. I think that Motown had the personnel to handle a performer like Florence Ballard and this I didn't know at the beginning. ABC was a huge [company] and had many talented people going to them, entertainers in the entertainment field."

Later in September, she shared the bill at the Auditorium

Theatre, Chicago, with Bill Cosby. Flo rode in a Chicago parade with comedian Godfrey Cambridge and received a good public response. Even the October birth of twin daughters Michelle and Nicole did not stop her plans for a new career. In one interview she did admit being a soloist was "kind of scary. I've never sung solo except in school, it's different and all. I'm a little nervous, but that's all, I hope." As for opening up about her departure from The Supremes, Flo was reluctant to discuss that topic as "something that just happened," or "that question."

On January 20, 1969, Flo sang at Richard Nixon's inaugural ball in Washington. After returning from the Washington festivities, Baun notified Flo that she was completely out of personal funds. The money released to him from the Motown agreement was gone. Flo Ballard went to his office on March 17, 1969 to collect all the documents relating to the Motown settlement; he released only part of them to her. Baun later notified her that he still had the $5,000 gift from The Supremes and other documents. On April 2, Flo terminated Baun's services as her attorney.

The frustration Flo experienced in attempting to piece together her personal life was complicating her singing career. ABC Records dropped the option on Flo Ballard's two year contract after the release of "Love Ain't Love". Plans were cancelled for the album release of YOU DON'T HAVE TO, although two dozen songs had been recorded. ABC executive Cynthia Sissle explained: "I think that they [ABC executives] thought they were getting a 'Supremes sound' when they signed the contract. They didn't have a Supremes singer. They had a good ballad singer." The company was not interested in picking up the option or releasing the album. Bateman stated: "After the single I did with her that was it....I think after that I am pretty sure what the situation was with her. When her contract was up they didn't pick up her up." [note: an album was produced as confirmed by MCA] It was dependent on the two singles to make it. "After that, like I said, it was coming up when I did that session on her, the close of her contract. It was coming up at that time, and I don't think they picked the option up."

In 1970 Florence began to open up a little about her career's failure: "Things looked good when I first started out as a single. I had signed with a new company and was pleased with the initial releases, and even had a few engagements lined up. Then all of a sudden it seemed as if I was blackballed. My records weren't played and there were no bookings. People would have come to see me out of curiosity alone that first year." She felt good to be recording again, her voice had not deteriorated, and George Kerr was producing. She met Larry Newton, the President of ABC on one occasion. He told her it was not good for an artist to switch recording companies. He also mentioned that he spoke with Berry Gordy on the golf course. Shortly afterward the company dropped its interest in her. "Love Ain't Love" was not distributed in Detroit. Her husband got some boxes of the single and distributed them in a few downtown stores and had it placed on WCHB, a black radio station in Detroit. She was told by many friends who heard her ABC recordings that they were good, but as she said, "Anybody can put out a record. You could go somewhere and record and put it out and that's about it. Nobody wants to play it but you."

A recording company's relationship with an artist is not always ideal. Companies may not risk an investment of time or money on a singer or group under contract. The case of singer Janis Ian is an example of an artist in conflict with the interests of the company. Ian's popularity came at the age of sixteen with the 1968 release of "Society's Child", a controversial song of interracial love. As the song gained popularity, due in part because of Leonard Bernstein's personal endorsement on national television, Verve Records put Ian on the tour circuit without a road manager. She did not have an accountant to handle royalties, investments, or taxes. Two years later, Ian owed back taxes and lost $200,000. "I thought I was rich, but that was all I had and there it went," Ian told Robert Spitz.

Ian abandoned her recording career for four years. She spent time thinking about all that she had been through; when her money was gone, she moved in with her mother. In 1973, Ian was ready to resume her career. Record companies she contacted did not want to sign her to more than a one single contract. She had been out of the field too long; if one single made it on the charts the company would be paid for the investment. If the single did not fair well, the loss would not affect the company with further obligation to Ian. Eventually, she signed with the full support of Columbia Records. She described Columbia's support: "You see, not only is it my career at stake, but it's Columbia's money. We work together, which is the really good thing about them. And they're class. They're not tacky. They don't say they're going to throw you a party and bring frankfurters, they do it because you need to have a party in a particular town and they invite the right people. They don't jive around. It's an amazing machine. Except, as an artist, you don't feel like it's a machine."

Florence Ballard did not have the support of ABC to help her resolve some of the problems that she faced in 1969. Blues singer Bo Diddley explained how he had been caught in these business problems. "When I first went out, I was hungry. I'd never had over $150 in my hand at one time and two or three hundred started looking good, you understand what I mean? A thousand? Oh, my god! You couldn't say nothing to me until I learned some sense. And this is what everybody at the record companies were doing to a lot of the entertainers. Then they drop you by the way-side when you least expect it, man. You might be deciding to go buy you and your family a home and you think everything is beautiful, man. All of a sudden a cat says, 'Well, we ain't gonna cut you,' or they cut you then stick your stuff on a shelf. Well, the only thing they do is fulfill the contract."

"You are out of it, every time you get a statement you owe them. Pretty soon when you catch up with it the word goes down the line, 'Don't touch him, cause he ain't no good.' That's the way it works. 'Who was you with last year? Well, why'd you leave?' [Reply] 'Well, we'll talk to you next week.' By the time you walk out the door, click, click, click, 'Hey man, what's with so and so?— Oh, bad news.' When you come back it's, 'Sorry, we can't do nothing for you today.' Pretty soon you can't play for a dog and cat show."

ABC Records had fulfilled the contract with Flo and her recordings were shelved. She never entered a recording studio after the Bateman sessions. "I always thought very highly of her artistic ability....Like I told Florence, they would have had to physically restrained me, really, I would be there with my own microphone and P.A. right there with them [The Supremes]....I just would not have....I did not know how she could have left that success. This is what I am saying. When they were performing, they could not get rid of me."

With the deterioration of her financial situation, Flo began searching for someone in the city of Detroit to handle her case so, she contacted the Wayne County Prosecutor's Office. Flo's brother, Willie Ballard, explained to Lieutenant Boggs the possible embezzlement of funds by Baun. Boggs advised Mr. Ballard that he would investigate the matter; nothing came of this meeting. Responding to a letter of complaint, the Detroit Police Department advised Miss Ballard to speak with assistant prosecutor Jay Nolan. Nolan disqualified himself from the case because of his friendship with Leonard Baun. He advised the Ballards to file a complaint with the Michigan State Bar Association.

Florence Ballard tried to retain the services of another attorney, but her efforts were unsuccessful. One attorney returned the retainer; another was a neighbor of Baun whose services she then terminated; two others felt the case was too big to handle. Another assistant prosecutor, Mike Connors, made an appointment to review her case on May 29, 1969, but he did not appear for the appointment. William Cain, also of the prosecutor's office, advised her to engage the services of Bernard Adams. Baun refused to turn over the documents to Adams.

For five months, Florence and Willie Ballard contacted The Federal Bureau of Investigation; The Attorney General Office, State of Michigan; The American Bar Association; The Internal Revenue Service; The Circuit Court of Wayne County; Senator Julian Bond; Congressman John Conyers; Representative James Del Rio; and The Bank of the Commonwealth. The Bank of the Commonwealth, where she had an account as a Supreme, would not give her any information regarding her Motown settlement without a subpoena.

Publicity on the former Supreme was featured in the papers in a series of articles. In the fall of 1968, Florence was featured in the *Detroit Free Press Sunday Magazine*. Her new career was the leading article complete with color photos. Although the interview revealed little on why Flo left The Supremes, Barbara Holliday did shed some light on Florence herself. The feature was supportive of Florence's efforts at re-establishing herself, as the Detroit papers had always been favorable to the Motown artists. Detroit was very proud of its artists. Again in the winter of 1969, Florence was interviewed favorably in *Ebony*. During the summer of 1969, a Canadian paper contacted Miss Holliday in Detroit to write a follow-up story on Flo. Florence was not available for an interview with the press unless there was payment. Further investigation revealed the problems she was having. The *Free Press* story "Former Supreme Suffers Long Fall From Stardom" described that "sentimental favorite" Supreme Flo was depressed, "flat broke" after she paid her taxes, and deserted by her husband. The Chapmans had turned down some lucrative offers in March 1969 when Michael Gussick, a former ABC attorney, approached Baun about some work for Florence. The article in the *Free Press* did not sit well with the Chapmans. On July 16, 1969 Tommy Chapman and Florence Ballard Chapman, represented by Bernard Adams, filed suit against the *Free Press* for a retraction and an apology. The suit stated that they had suffered character defamation and were asking $10 million in damages. More than a year later on October 12, 1970, the suit against the *Free Press* was dropped when no progress was made and the paper refused to retract the article.

A few months after the Chapmans filed suit, the *Free Press* broke the story that Diana Ross would leave Mary Wilson and Cindy Birdsong for a solo career in January. Prior speculation in the gossip columns by Detroiter Shirley Eder had inferred that Flo was being considered to replace Miss Ross in The Supremes. Berry Gordy's response was that the chemistry had to be right for the replacement. This hopeful dream of many of Flo's "sentimental" fans was put to rest when Motown announced that Jean Terrell would be the new lead singer of The Supremes.

Former WXYZ Radio personality Lee Allen, who had been part of that early Motown record hop scene, ran a special "Supremes" show late in November of 1969 discussed the change in the group. "Of course it wasn't very long ago when The Supremes split the first time when Florence Ballard left The Supremes. She is here in Detroit now, she is no longer a member of The Supremes, she left to improve her career evidently, and so far it has not happened. She is a tremendous person and a tremendous personality, but maybe leaving The Supremes was the jinx, you know, who knows. A lot of people have left the Motown organization and we haven't heard of them again, Mary Wells is one of them, and it goes on, and on, and on." Although requested, Allen did not play Flo's single on his show. Producer Robert Bateman who, with Mary Wells, left Motown: "Until recently, I don't know how to term recently, until recently, early days, I don't think anyone who left Motown had much success. I think they [Motown] had such a stronghold they could stop whomever they wanted to stop."

Florence retained the law firm of Patmon, Young and Kirk in September 1969 to investigate her settlement with Motown. In her deposition for the Wayne County Circuit Court, Flo maintained that after the attorneys investigated the settlement, she was informed that Motown Records had concealed monies from her attorney, which were due her. The civil action of Flo Ballard versus Motown, Gordy and Ross did not come before the court until October 1970.

Flo's new attorney, Gerald Dent, worked for two and half years on her case and appeal against both Motown and Baun. He prepared the hours of deposition which are a part of this case study. Gerald Dent was previously a Saginaw, Michigan assistant prosecutor. An associate of his described the 36 year old Dent as "a brilliant criminal attorney, very intelligent, but very high-strung." Dent had been indicted in September, 1971, by a Wayne County Citizens' Grand Jury on an obstruction of justice charge for allegedly persuading a witness in a narcotic case to hide in Canada. Charges against him were dropped when the witness refused to testify against Dent.

On Monday, April 2, 1973, [now] Judge James Del Rio and Johnette Dent spoke for an hour and a half. Mrs. Dent informed Del Rio that her husband had tried to kill himself the day before using pills. The couple had been having marital problems which had started to affect his law practice. The previous Friday, Dent failed to appear in [now] Judge Michael O'Connor's court. During the day on Tuesday, Dent congratulated Patrolman James Harris, formerly a STRESS officer on his return to the regular forces. Dent criticized the STRESS program [Stop the Robberies Enjoy Safe Streets] telling Harris, "All they [STRESS] do is kill black people." The STRESS program had come under public criticism for being trigger happy. Dent was professional until late that afternoon after receiving two upsetting phone calls. Brady Denton, a Saginaw prosecutor, had spoken to Dent regarding the retrial on a murder case in which Dent had made a cross examination error. This case had been the first one in his legal career. He was scheduled to make a court appearance for the retrial because of his familiarity with the case. Before entering Del Rio's court on Tuesday afternoon, the Judge asked Dent if everything was going to be all right, Dent responded, "yes."

In a bizarre courtroom drama, Dent pulled a .38 snub nosed revolver from his coat. Dent pointed the gun at his own head, then aimed it at Judge James Del Rio, then turned to the police officer on the stand, Officer Worobec. A flurry of bullets rang through the courtroom, Dent was killed by a Detroit Police officer. Ironically the gun had been reported stolen during a break-in in Detroit's fashionable black and white mixed neighborhood of Palmer Park. The officer on the stand was testifying against three person charged with carrying concealed weapons and resisting arrest, Dent's client's. Judge Del Rio would not say who fired first; however, court recorder Myron DiBartolomo said that Dent did. Judge Del Rio blamed the Police Commissioner John Nichols for not providing more security in the courtroom. Judge Del Rio felt that if one more officer had been present, Dent could have been disarmed.

Prior to his death, Dent had left the law firm and was handling Flo's case on his own. However, after this tragedy, Florence returned to the firm and yet another attorney, David Tate, tried to piece together the evidence that Dent had amassed over two and a half years.

The $8.5 million suit was dismissed by the Circuit Court and the dismissal was upheld by The Michigan Supreme Court. The General Release was legally binding unless Florence Ballard could tender back to Motown the original $160,000 settlement. This, of course, was not possible because Baun had co-mingled her estate with his own. She filed a suit against Baun which was settled in her favor after the Michigan State Bar Association disbarred Baun.

Florence's nightmare life continued for nine years. She had stopped singing in 1969. Her on and off marriage was back on and in 1973 she gave birth to her third daughter, Lisa. Preoccupied, depressed, Florence was under physicians' care during all this time and yet she did occasionally make appearances. She saw The Supremes perform at the Elmwood Casino several times. When Flo attended a birthday party for one of Diana Ross's daughters in Berry Gordy's Boston Boulevard mansion in the mid-1970s, her dry humor was intact. When Miss Ross sang "Happy Birthday", Flo remarked to a reporter, "She's singing flat." In 1973 she lost her home on West Buena Vista through foreclosure.

In 1974 Florence made a trip to the West Coast to see Mary Wilson. During that visit, The Supremes, Scherrie Payne, Cindy Birdsong and Mary Wilson appeared at Magic Mountain. When Mary announced Florence Ballard, the crowd roared. Flo made a halting first time appearance as a Supreme since that fateful night in Las Vegas seven summers earlier. She told Detroit newscaster Dave Diles on The Lou Gordon Show, "I still love listening to the records. It took me a long time to want to listen to them ....I had mental anguish and a whole bunch of other mental problems. It was bitterness, and just hearing the records, I guess I wanted to still be there and I couldn't and it seemed to just, in other words, tear me up inside."

After returning to Detroit from the trip, her situation deteriorated. Personally shattered, financially ruined, professionally locked-out of entertainment, the once proud Florence Ballard applied for welfare. This news hit the papers like a thunderbolt. The success of The Supremes, Diana Ross, and Motown made Flo's fall from stardom even more devastating. She once described her life as being on a fast moving train that suddenly stopped. "I've been through, like I said, a lot of mental anguish and I've been to doctors and I've spent my life trying to come out of this nightmare. It seemed to me like I was dreaming, that this was just a horrible dream," she explained to Diles. "I kept saying to myself, well at least couldn't I have just kept my home if nothing else? For my children's sake, couldn't that at least have been paid for. I mean the question kept going through my mind and I would just break up inside." However, she did seem determined to get her life going again. In February she made some non-singing appearances in the Motor City, appeared on television, and talked about putting a show together.

In the summer of 1975, the case against Baun was settled and Flo received a settlement of approximately $50,000. She and her family moved into a new home in northwest Detroit. She seemed happier and wanted to provide for her family. She told Diles about her daughters. "They're beautiful, but then I think all children are. They can do the 'bump,' and I can't! The baby is two years old and the twins will be seven this year. But I don't know. I guess I was like that too as a child."

On June 25, 1975 Florence Ballard made her first concert appearance to an adoring hometown crowd in Detroit's Henry and Edsel Ford Auditorium. The event was a benefit for the Joan Little Defense League. Ms. Little was on trial in North Carolina for the murder of a guard who had raped her. The fund raiser also featured Lily Tomlin [another Detroiter], Gloria Steinem, and others. Florence was nervous about the show and very quiet backstage according to Deadly Nightshade band member Helen Hooke. Knowing that Florence was going to be on the show, the band rehearsed a number of Supremes' tunes. When it came time to perform Florence insisted upon performing "I Am Woman," the song made popular by Helen Reddy. The band obliged, and Florence Ballard was back in full control in the packed auditorium. The applause came in waves and they demanded an encore, a Supremes' encore. The Deadly Nightshade came through with "Come See About Me," and Florence was home, on stage in Detroit.

The future was bright enough that summer night and through the fall, but again it was an elusive star that followed Florence. On Saturday, February 21, 1976 she collapsed at home and was rushed to Mt. Carmel Mercy Hospital. Florence had been fighting high blood pressure, overweight and depression for years. The toll was too great for the girl who sang her heart out as one of America's Sweethearts, early on Sunday morning, February 22, 1976, Flo died. The medical report attributed her death to cardiac arrest, but one teary eyed mourner put it best: "That child died of a broken heart." Flo was only thirty two. Motown paid for the funeral expenses, and Diana Ross set up a trust fund for Flo's daughters. Flo left behind her twin daughters aged 7, a baby daughter aged 3 and a nation of "old teenagers."

"They're great and they always will be. I'm one of their greatest fans. But the best part was back at the beginning. Some one of these days, maybe we'll jump up together and sing again, just for the fun of it! We were all sad when I left, I knew I had to get some rest. It didn't last too long. We were bound, someday, to go our separate ways..."
Florence Ballard

Chapter VII
Summary

Florence Ballard began her singing career as an equal with her partners Mary Wilson and Diana Ross. Each of the girls came from the same background, had the same opportunity, and talent. The dedication Berry Gordy had for the group and his efforts to make them professional entertainers was evident; Ballard, Wilson, and Ross became internationally recognized stars. Although Ballard formed the group and chose its name, Ross was made the focal point of The Supremes under Gordy's direction. This did contribute to misunderstandings and jealousies among the members of the group. Despite Ross's preferential treatment, Ballard and Wilson did benefit from Gordy's guidance.

The Supremes' performance reviews were good in 1967, but problems affected the group, some of which are yet unknown publicly. To maintain the momentum of the continued achievements of The Supremes, and ultimately his company, Gordy had to resolve the conflict. Florence Ballard, as any entertainer, was replaceable. Talent was not reason enough for her to remain with The Supremes; Cindy Birdsong could effectively replace Flo Ballard without the conflicts. As Gordy indicated, correcting the small problems prevents trouble. The dismissal of Flo from The Supremes was a business decision.

Flo Ballard had the talent to be a solo artist even before the years of training and experience as a Supreme at Motown. The release of Florence from the company was a loss for both. Motown had made an investment in her artistic capabilities which could not be fulfilled, and Flo Ballard lost the direction she needed. Perhaps if she had remained with Motown Records, her desire to perform alone would have been realized.

Entertainers beginning their careers need assistance with the artistic elements of the entertainment industry. Florence Ballard left Motown as a member of a group; she did not have the experience of performing as a soloist. Upon leaving Motown the responsibility of artist development by way of sound management was her own. ABC Records did not make a practice of building recording acts as Motown had built The Supremes; unfortunately, Flo required more guidance than ABC provided.

Entertainers also demand promotion to be commercially successful. Florence's efforts toward establishing herself as a singer for ABC were stalled by the prohibition of using the Supremes' name in reference to her own artistic promotion. She was publicly known as a background singer; Ballard's talent as a solo artist was not identified. Flo Ballard was not known individually; she was a Supreme. After the name change to "Diana Ross and the Supremes," Ross gained the needed name recognition for her solo career. If ABC Records had been able to use the promotional phrase "The Supremes' Florence Ballard," her artistic promotion may have been enhanced and she would have gotten more attention. This restriction on publicity by Motown Records prevented ABC from advancing Flo without further investment. The two singles were a test of how well her name was recognized.

In the recording industry record sales were the criteria which determined the viability of an artist's profession. Even in Detroit, where Florence Ballard was known, her single, "Love Ain't Love," was not available in metropolitan area stores due to insufficient sales promotion. Radio stations used sales figures as an indication of a song's popularity before the song was placed on the playlists. Unlike Motown, ABC could not and did not aggressively promote this record's sales. Major radio outlets such as CKLW in Detroit used regional and national sales figures before choosing songs for air play. Without this promotion, Ballard's releases were not played and as a result did not sell. In addition to the limits of ABC's promotion, hometown press publicity about Flo was not possible. The *Detroit Free Press* and the *Detroit News* were on strike for the nine months that Florence Ballard recorded for ABC. The papers had been very supportive of The Supremes; if the papers had been operating, Flo Ballard would have received publicity. The public was not fully aware a change had occurred in The Supremes or that Florence had started a solo career. The 1969 lawsuit against the *Free Press* did nothing to further endear her to the hometown press.

The complexities of the entertainment industry, as a business, necessitated the artist's reliance on ethical representation. Flo Ballard was assured of receiving financial guidance and legal assistance when she was associated with Motown Records. After leaving Motown, she placed her faith for these services in attorney Leonard Baun. Baun violated the confidence and trust of this position. Furthermore, his handling of Flo Ballard's finances was inconsistent with the requirement of the Michigan law. Less than one year after the $160,000 Motown settlement, Florence was without money.

The competitive situation which Flo Ballard referred to between Motown Records and ABC Records has not been verified. However by changing recording companies, she created a situation where two competitors had recordings by her. If Motown had unreleased recordings of Ballard which could be released to compete with the marketing of Flo's ABC recordings, Motown could promote Flo as a Supreme and take advantage of this competitive edge on ABC's investment. Motown, of course, was promoting Diana Ross for her solo career and not interested in bringing any publicity to Florence. Simultaneously, Flo's legal problems with Baun became more confused. Perhaps ABC, aware of Baun's mismanagement, was reluctant to involve itself with Florence Ballard. Conducting business with Baun could have resulted in financial and legal liabilities for ABC. Under these circumstances the company's desire to invest in Ballard became less attractive. ABC fulfilled the contractual obligation to record Ballard, and the recordings were shelved. The rest of her life was monopolized with untangling this web of problems.

The ABC contract and recordings were transferred to MCA/Universal when the music division was sold. According to one MCA vice-president, if MCA chose to release the Florence Ballard recordings, the restrictions of the original contracts would stand. Interest in releasing Flo's records has been expressed throughout the years especially with the popularity of DREAMGIRLS. Florence was the prototype for the leading character in this Tony Award-winning musical.

The case of Florence Ballard documents an incident with one entertainer in the recording industry. The results of this study bring forth additional questions regarding Ballard and the profession in general. The following issues were not addressed, but provide a basis for future research. Therefore, these questions are proposed: To what extent does Florence Ballard's experience occur in the entertainment business as a whole? Was her situation unique or common?

The effective business management of entertainers is dependent on a mutual understanding of shared goals of the artist and the company. Motown forfeited its investment in Florence Ballard by dismissing her, and Florence sacrificed her livelihood as a result. Could Motown and Ballard have resolved their problems more effectively? To what extent does the entertainment industry squander the resources of talent when these misunderstandings occur?

Conducting a case study presents special problems for research. The documentation of events years after the fact may be an obstacle to overcome. Business implications of artist changing record companies, artist-management conflicts, and blacklisting of entertainers all relate to this type of study. In this study a review of the literature revealed no information which dealt exclusively with Florence Ballard or The Supremes except in primary sources. These primary sources of information were utilized to reconstruct an overview of Ballard's professional life. The documents of Ballard's lawsuit against Motown were located in the Circuit Court of Wayne County. In addition to the literature, personal interviews and interviews from radio and television furnished another important source of information. The sensitive nature of Ballard's problems also made some of the people less willing to divulge information. Discretion was an important element in this research.

Was Florence the victim of wrongdoing? Certainly her career was mismanaged by Baun; by acting upon the advice of others, and her own misjudgments, Florence's dismissal from Motown was a mistake. Mary Wilson talked about the profession and what is needed: "One of the main problems I found in our career was that most entertainers or people in the entertainment business are not aware of the business aspects of it. This is one of the most important areas that you should always be concerned with because that really constitutes you future. Your earnings ability and if you are not aware it is very possible you could earn money and not even know what you are earning. I would say that is one of the main things for anyone starting out or even those in the business to find people you can trust to handle it and to let you know what they are making. Trust." Robert Bateman on Flo's career: "I always thought very highly of her artistic ability. Now, a lot of times an artist's personal guidance is not there. You know, like whoever you have acting as your manager or your consultant or your advisor. A lot of the artists were ill-advised."

Or was it Florence herself, the Quiet Supreme with the talent for an enigmatic smile? As Rosilee Trombley explained, "I would say that Florence Ballard probably ended up being Florence Ballard's worst enemy. There are a lot of them who cannot deal with success....So I would think that Florence probably had a hard time with success and Berry Gordy was a very strict mentor...."

Diana Ross talked a little about Florence shortly after her death for the *Detroit Free Press*. "The problems were mainly in her head. She was tired, she didn't love what she was doing. She wanted out, Florence was buying a lot of furs and fancy cars, but she wasn't having fun....If I had known how it was going to end with Florence maybe I would have taken more time with her."

Florence Ballard was a talented singer and a dynamic performer, but she did not understand the business. It was not enough that she had this desire to sing; she had to conform to the business as did Diana Ross and Mary Wilson. Berry Gordy had a penchant for choosing winners. He chose The Supremes but not every Supreme was a winner. Gordy lost one of his best artists; The Supremes' aura of three Detroit girls rising from rags to riches like modern day Cinderellas was gone after Florence was dropped from the trio; and ABC Records forfeited an opportunity to create a new star. And the fans, for whom The Supremes have now become a part of the collective conscience of a generation, lost Florence. But Florence Ballard lost everything and that was the tragedy.

The Supremes
(l-r) Diana Ross, Mary Wilson, Florence Ballard

SELECTED BIBLIOGRAPHY
BOOKS

Benjaminson, Peter. *The Story of Motown.* New York: Grove Press, Inc., 1979.

Betrock, Alan. *Girl Groups: The Story of a Sound.* New York: Delilah Books, 1982.

Davis, Clive. *Clive: Inside the Recording Business.* New York: W. Morrow, 1975.

Faulk, John Henry. *Fear on Trial.* New York: Simon and Shuster, 1964.

Fornatale, Peter and Joshua Mills. *Radio in the Television Age.* Woodstock, New York: Overlook Press, 1980.

Hall, Claude and Barbara Hall. *This Business of Radio Programming.* New York: Billboard Publications, 1977.

Haskins, James. *I'm Gonna Make You Love Me: The Story of Diana Ross.* New York: Dell Publishing Company, 1980.

Morse, David. *Motown and the Arrival of Black Music.* London: Studio Vista, 1971.

Osgoode, Dick. *WYXIE Wonderland: An Unauthorized 50 Year Diary of WXYZ Detroit.* Bowling Green, Ohio: Bowling Green University Popular Press, 1981.

Redd, Lawrence. *Rock is Rhythm and Blues.* East Lansing, Michigan: Michigan State University Press, 1974.

Shemel, Sidney and William Krasilovsky. *This Business of Music.* New York: Billboard Publications, 1977.

Spitz, Robert S. *The Making of Superstars: The Artists and the Executives of the Rock Music Business.* Garden City,

71

New York: Anchor Press/Doubleday Books, 1978.

Stokes, Geoffrey. *Star Making Machinery: The Odyssey of an Album.* New York: The Bobbs-Merrill Company, 1976.

Vaughn, Robert. *Only Victims.* New York: 1972.

Whitburn, Joel. *Top Pop Records, 1955-1970.* Detroit: Gale Research Company, 1971.

Periodicals

Billboard Magazine. 10 February 1968.
_____ 13 April 1968.
_____ 11 May 1968.

Brown, Stanley H. "The Motown Sound of Money." *Fortune,* September 1, 1967, p. 103.

"Former Supreme Talks—A Little: Florence Ballard Maintains Secrecy About Trio's Split-up." *Ebony,* February 1969, p. 83.

Hamilton, Jack. "The Supremes: From Real Rags to Real Riches." *Look,* May 3, 1966, pp.70-76.

Miller, Edwin. "Off the Record with the Supremes." *Seventeen,* August 1966, pp. 280.

Tiegl, Eliot. "Motown Expansion in High with Broadway, TV, Movies." *Billboard,* June 11, 1966, p. 1.

Documents

"A Confidential Report for The Music and Radio Industries, Number 5." Digest of Song Charts, April 15, 1972, p. 1.

Ypsilanti, Michigan. Eastern Michigan University. The Motown Papers.

Detroit. Wayne County Circuit Court. Civil Action 173-853, Ballard vs. Ross, et al.
_____ General Release
_____ Second Recording Agreement, Exhibit "B"
_____ Supplemental Agreement, July 26, 1967.
_____ Deposition of Florence Ballard Chapman p/k/a/ Florence Ballard, May 6, 1971.

U.S. Congress. Senate. Senator Philip A. Hart. Testimony to Berry Gordy, Jr. before the Senate. 92nd Cong., 1st sess., 19 April 1971. Congressional Record, vol 117.

Selected Articles

"Florence Ballard: The New Life of An Ex-Supreme," *Detroit Free Press Magazine*, 20 October 1968, pp. 14-21.

"Former Supreme Suffers Long Fall From Stardom," *Detroit Free Press*, 11 July 1969, pp. A1-2.

"Cindy Birdsong: Fourth (and Last?) of the Supremes." *Detroit Free Press Magazine*, 13 April 1969, pp. 24-31.

"A Solo for Diana," *Detroit Free Press*, 2 November 1969, pp. A1-2.

"Ex-Supreme Leads a Forgotten Life," *Detroit Free Press*, 17 January 1975, p. A1.

"Ex-Supreme Florence Ballard is Dead," *Detroit Free Press*, 23 February 1975, p. A3.

"The Supremes Set the Record Straight," *Detroit News: Tempo*, 31 August 1967, p.10.

"Supremes, 5,000 At Flo's Rites," *Detroit News*, 28 February, 1975, p. A1.

"Peace of Mind is the 'Supreme' Sacrifice for Florence Ballard," *Michigan Chronicle*, 14 November 1970, p. B7.

"Ex-Supreme Sues Law Firm for 7.5 Million," *Michigan Chronicle*, 14 November 1970, p. A1.

"Last Supreme Sues Motown: Mary Wilson is Disgruntled," *Michigan Chronicle*, 31 December 1977, p. A1.

"The Big, Happy Beating Heart of the Detroit Sound," *New York Times Magazine*, 27 November 1966, pp. 48.

"The Super Supremes: Stop! In the Name of Love," *New York Times*, 23 July 1967, p. D11.

Discography

Florence Ballard

ABC Records # 11074 "It Doesn't Matter How I Say It (It Is What I Say That Matters) b/w "Goin' Out Of My Head" produced by George Kerr, 1968.

ABC Records # 11144 "Love Ain't Love" b/w "Forever Faithful" produced by Robert Bateman, 1968.

You Don't Have To [unreleased album in MCA archives] 1968.

Kent Records, Ace Records, Inc., 1983. *Soul Class of 1966* [Anthology] "Love Ain't Love"

Florence Ballard with the Supremes

Motown Records:

"Buttered Popcorn" *Meet the Supremes*, 1964.
"It Makes No Difference Now" *Country Western & Pop*, 1964.
"Ain't That Good News" *We Remember Sam Cooke*, 1964.
"Manhattan" *Diana Ross and the Supremes 25th Anniversary*, 1986.
"Save Me A Star" and
"Silent Night" *The Never Before Released Masters*, compact disc, 1987.

Looking Back

Dowtown Detroit looking north. The J.L. Hudson Department Store rises 25 stories above Woodward Avenue on the right, 1965. Like much of Detroit, this corner is now empty; Hudson's, Kern's and Sam's have been demolished. Motown Records left in the early '70. Below Florence, Diana and Mary pose like Grecian muses.

Florence, Mary, Diana performing in the early years, above left, and on British Television, above right. [courtesy of Thomas Ingrassia]

The signs of success, limo rides and a fur-wrapped return to the Brewster Projects in Detroit, circa 1965.

Florence, Bobby Darrin, Diana and Mary singing on the television special,
"Anatomy of Pop" in 1966. Mary, Diana and Florence are at the hands of the
legendary Richard Rodgers prior to recording the album
The Supremes Sing Rodgers and Hart.
[courtesy of Thomas Ingrassia]

Looking sharp on television in 1966. [courtesy of Thomas Ingrassia]

Florence following a performance, above. (courtesy of Doug Wright)

Florence in Detroit at a store display of Supreme white bread, 1966.

Mary, Diana and Florence get a special greeting from the Shriners of Philadelphia in April, 1967.
[courtesy of Thomas Ingrassia]

Florence in Philadelphia in 1967
[courtesy of Thomas Ingrassia]

Florence at ABC Records,
1968.

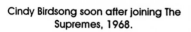

Cindy Birdsong soon after joining The
Supremes, 1968.

Flo's last record release at ABC and Detroit Free Press writer Barbara Holliday's follow-up article in the summer of 1969 when Florence's solo career was grinding to a halt.

Former Supreme Suffers Long Fall from Stardom

BY BARBARA HOLLIDAY
Free Press Staff Writer

Ex-Supreme Florence Ballard Chapman, a sentimental favorite with her fans, has fallen on bad times.

The run of bad luck which began two years ago when she was dropped from Motown's famous singing group — due to her health, she said — is still with her.

A source close to the singer says she is living in seclusion in her northwest Detroit home on Buena Vista with her infant twin daughters. She was reportedly deserted by her husband, Tommy Chapman, and has been advised by her attorney that she is "flat broke."

Florence's last public appearance was last January. She was one of the entertainers invited to the Nixon inaugural events. Since then, she has withdrawn more and more from friends and associates.

Florence also has filed charges with the Michigan State Bar against one of her attorneys, Leonard A. Baun. Baun says Florence charged him with mismanagement of her funds, but calls

Turn to Page 2A, Column 1

EX-SUPREME Florence Ballard Chapman in 1966, when she was riding high.

Hitsville, USA, 1982, now it is a
museum and historic site.
[courtesy of Linda Champion]

The Detroit gang
Thomas Ingrassia, Mary Wilson,
Linda Champion, and Gary Oleszko,
following Mary's BEEHIVE
performance in Windsor, Ontario,
1989.
[courtesy of Thomas Ingrassia]

Two old teens: Randall
Wilson with the supreme
Mary Wilson in Danville,
California, 1998.
[courtesy of Jon Chusid]

Mary Wilson at a book signing in San Francisco, 1986.

FLORENCE BALLARD DISCOGRAPHY, 1998 by Gil Lucero and Dan Verona

SUPREMES RECORDINGS

RECORDING	LEAD, FEATURED OR STAND-OUT VOCAL	YEAR	ALBUM LOCATION	SINGLE RELEASE? (A/B)
"Tears Of Sorrow"	STAND-OUT	1960	"LOOKING BACK WITH THE PRIMETTES & EDDIE FLOYD"	C D / L P ONLY
"Pretty Baby"	STAND-OUT	1960	"LOOKING BACK WITH THE PRIMETTES & EDDIE FLOYD"	C D / L P ONLY
"Save Me A Star"	LEAD	1961	"THE NEVER-BEFORE RELEASED MASTERS" (CD - 1987)	NO
"Buttered Popcorn"	LEAD	1961	"MEET THE SUPREMES" (1963)	YES (A)
"Let Me Go The Right Way"	STAND-OUT	1962	"MEET THE SUPREMES" (1963)	YES (A)
"It Makes No Difference Now"	FEATURED	1963	"SING COUNTRY WESTERN & POP" (1965)	NO
"The Man With The Rock and Roll Banjo Band"	STAND-OUT	1963	"SING COUNTRY WESTERN & POP" (1965)	YES (B)
"Mr. Blues"	FEATURED	1963	"THE NEVER-BEFORE RELEASED MASTERS" (CD - 1987)	NO
"A Breathtaking Guy"	FEATURED	1963	"WHERE DID OUR LOVE GO" (1964)	YES (A)
"Long Gone Lover"	FEATURED	1963	"WHERE DID OUR LOVE GO" (1964)	NO
"Come On Boy"	STAND-OUT	1963	"25ᵗʰ ANNIVERSARY" (CD - 1986)	NO
"Penny Pincher"	STAND-OUT	1964	"25ᵗʰ ANNIVERSARY (CD - 1986)	NO
"Remove This Doubt"	STAND-OUT	1964	"SING HOLLAND-DOZIER-HOLLAND" (1966)	YES (B)
"Who Could Ever Doubt My Love"	STAND-OUT	1964	"MORE HITS BY THE SUPREMES" (1965)	YES (B)
"Cupid"	STAND-OUT	1965	"WE REMEMBER SAM COOKE" (1965)	NO
"(Ain't That) Good News"	LEAD	1965	"WE REMEMBER SAM COOKE" (1965)	NO
"(Love Is Like A) Heat Wave" (MONO)	STAND-OUT	1965	"SING HOLLAND-DOZIER-HOLLAND" (1966)	NO
"Sleepwalk"	STAND-OUT	1965	"25ᵗʰ ANNIVERSARY" (CD - 1986)	NO
"It's All Your Fault"	STAND-OUT	1965	"25ᵗʰ ANNIVERSARY" (CD - 1986)	NO
"Sincerely"	STAND-OUT	1965	"25ᵗʰ ANNIVERSARY" (CD - 1986)	NO
"Silent Night" (abbreviated version)	LEAD	1965	"THE NEVER-BEFORE-RELEASED MASTERS" (CD - 1987)	NO

"Silent Night" (orchestrated, full version)	LEAD	1965	"CHRISTMAS IN THE CITY" (CD - 1993)	NO
"We Couldn't Get Along Without You" (Special lyrics to "My World Is Empty Without You")	STAND-OUT	1966	"25th ANNIVERSARY" (CD - 1986)	NO
"Fancy Passes"	FEATURED	1966	"THE NEVER-BEFORE RELEASED MASTERS" (CD - 1987)	NO
"Misery Makes It's Home In My Heart"	STAND-OUT	1966	"REFLECTIONS" (1968)	NO
"Manhattan"	FEATURED	1966	"THE RODGERS & HART COLLECTION" (CD - 1987)	NO
"You Keep Me Hangin' On"	STAND-OUT	1966	"SING HOLLAND-DOZIER-HOLLAND" (1966)	YES (A)
"The Ballad of Davy Crockett"	FEATURED	1967	"THE NEVER-BEFORE RELEASED MASTERS" (CD - 1987)	NO
"Whistle While You Work"	FEATURED	1967	"THE NEVER-BEFORE RELEASED MASTERS" (CD - 1987)	NO

ABC RECORDS - SOLO

A-SIDE	B-SIDE	LABEL #	YEAR	PIC SLEEVE?
"It Doesn't Matter How I Say It (It's What I Say That Matters)"	"Goin' Out Of My Head"	ABC-11074	1968	NO
"Love Ain't Love"	"Forever Faithful"	ABC-11144	1968	YES

"YOU DON'T HAVE TO", (1968
ABC RECORDS LP - UNRELEASED)
"You Don't Have To"
"Like You, Babe"
"Yesterday"
"Until Tomorrow"
"It's Not Unusual"
"Forever Faithful"
"It Doesn't Matter How I Say It
(It's What I Say That Matters)"
"Let's Stay In Love"
"Walk On By"
"Goin' Out Of My Head"
"Sweetness"
"Everything Wonderful"
"Love Ain't Love"

Additional Tracks
"The Impossible Dream"
"My Heart"
"You Love Me"

Solo CD Appearances
"It Doesn't Matter How I Say It
(It's What I Say That Matters)"
"SOULFUL DIVAS, VOL.1 -
Pop 'n' Soul Sirens"
Hippo Records, ©1998
HIPD40094